GOLF
– THE PRO'S DON'T
KNOW IT ALL

BY NEILL WATSON KERR

BIELDSIDE PUBLISHING
ABERDEEN, SCOTLAND

GOLF
– THE PRO'S DON'T
KNOW IT ALL

BY NEILL WATSON KERR

ISBN 0-953-18250-9

First Published in Great Britain
by Bieldside Publishing 1998

Conditions of Sale

Set in Times by Harley & Cox Ltd.

Printed and bound by Harley & Cox Ltd., Dundee, Scotland

LIST OF CONTENTS

FOREWORD
by JOHN CHILLAS

Professional at Glenbervie Golf Club
Former Scottish Professional and Matchplay Champion

I have been coaching golf for more than 25 years and thought I knew practically everything about the golf swing and how it functions. In that time I have come across many pupils who were very gifted and their game only required a few refinements to put them back on course. Equally, I have had pupils who have not responded particularly well to tuition. Having read Neill Kerr's book I now understand why the latter sometimes struggle to come to terms with the game of golf.

The book at no stage suggests there is a perfect way for everyone to swing the club. Instead, Neill concentrates on analysing the body functions both skeletal and muscular required to make what might be described as a functional golf swing. Each movement has been carefully analysed and easily explained.

Following the general principles in the book, I believe, will assist the average player acquire a more effective and reliable golf swing. Good players will also benefit by understanding how the body and limbs work within the golf swing.

Personally, I have learnt a great deal and am sure many of my fellow professionals will do likewise. Hopefully I can pass this information on to my own pupils.

At a time when many leading golf teachers seek alternative methods of striving to attain a consistent swing, Neill Kerr has shown in his book the importance of first of all understanding the basic principles of anatomical movement. He is to be congratulated on a simple but logical approach.

JOHN CHILLAS.

Scottish Professional Champion 1976
Scottish Matchplay Champion 1990
Represented GB & I v USA .... 1982, '83, '84, '88 & '92
Represented Scotland in European Club Professionals' Team Championship
(4 times)

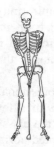

Introduction

Setting the Scene

Why do club golfers remain individuals perpetually struggling with their game and only rarely producing a fleeting glimpse of perfection? Why are we so incapable of raising our standards on to a higher plane? Our present day golf professionals are extremely skilled at their jobs and teaching standards are improving all the time. There is uniformity of method, video and mechanical trainers are available and there are hundreds, if not thousands, of books on the shelves that have been written by the best golfing gurus in the game. All aspects of the game have been analysed, the swing itself, the techniques of the short game, the skills of the long game, the arts of pitching and putting and even the deeper psychological aspects of the game. Why does this abundance of experience and advice bear so little fruit with the average club golfer?

One can hazard a few guesses as to why this might have been the case in the past where golf tuition was a rather unreliable and haphazard affair. Professionals had little training as teachers and much of their advice was conflicting. One professional might advocate dominance of the left side of the body throughout the swing, another might emphasise the thrust of the right knee or the right hand action. Back with the left and through with the right was common advice. Another might suggest gripping the club as lightly as possible while his colleague in the club next door might encourage a firm grip. Some encouraged a closed stance for the drive, some a square stance and others even suggested an open stance. Some eminent golfers started their swings with their hips, others with their shoulders, others with their wrists. Until recently there has been a great diversity of opinion about golf technique and teaching methods.

This is now behind us. Today we see much more uniformity, whether it be by the written word, on video, or as advice on the practice ground. Why then do we not see any great leap forward in expertise by the average club golfer, outwith the advantages that improved equipment has brought?

A difficult question to answer, but a look at the professionals themselves (especially the older ones) may provide us with a few clues. It is obvious that many professionals do conform to the classic concepts, but by no means all. Many depart from the accepted norms in their own swings and of the modern, or recent modern, players such as Brewer, Trevino, Hubert Green, Casper, Aoki, Darcy, Rafferty and Furyk, all are tournament golfers who possess less than classic swings, but yet are, or were in their day, top class golfers. It is possible to go even further back in time and look at pictures of the great Harry Vardon, three time winner of the Open Championship and see about the most bent left arm at the top of the swing it is possible to imagine. Maybe we should whisper it quietly – even the greatest golfer of all time has his flying right elbow! It would seem the list of golfing greats who indulge, or have indulged, in swing aberrations is almost endless and it would perhaps not be too far from the truth to suggest that almost every principle that has been formulated as being a basic ingredient of a good swing, has been broken by some golfer somewhere and yet that golfer has been capable of earning a great deal of money on the tournament circuits of the world.

It would therefore seem we have some inconsistencies in golf theory, and while I would agree that these "non-conformist" swings are on the decrease and an ever increasing number of modern tournament players are moving towards a classic mould, nevertheless, it cannot be denied that many unconventional swings do exist and they can function exceedingly well.

This raises the question as to whether it is a sensible aim to attempt to make all golfers conform to one swing technique, or should we not be attempting to find the correct swing technique to fit with each of us as an individual? Or, is this making the game too complex?

Many of us try exceedingly hard to emulate our idols. We seek advice, we read about the principles of the swing and we practise until the blisters appear. Rarely is all this effort blessed with success, and the

Holy Grail of length and accuracy seems, for most of us, to remain tantalisingly just beyond our reach. The gap between knowledge, hard work and ability seems never to close. Most of us know reasonably well what we ought to do, we often feel we are doing it, but rarely do we actually do it, far less retain it. Therefore, it would seem that, neither the experts in their writings, nor the teaching professionals on the practice ground, nor even the ardent golfer by his own self dedication is able successfully to close the gap between knowledge and action. Perhaps more disconcertingly, no really satisfactory explanation has ever been given to the average club golfer as to why he is so incompetent, almost regardless of the amount of hard work he puts in.

The title of this book my appear to be a rather arrogant one – I assure the reader it is certainly not intended to be. The book is written and aimed to fill what I feel is a gap in golf literature. It is an attempt to explain to the club golfer why he is so incompetent, and why the professionals and top amateurs are so good. I hope that, armed with this knowledge, the club golfer will be able to go back to his Professional and use the information in this book to his advantage and the two of them together can do something about closing the gap between the instructional advice and the pupil's apparent inability to carry out this advice on the golf course. My book is therefore essentially for the handicap golfer, the player who knows a fair bit about the basics of the game, the player who has tried advice, has tried lessons and has tried to analyse his or her game but has not achieved the success they desire. My researches over the years have led me to believe that most fit and healthy individuals, who wish to put some effort into practice and intelligent analysis of their game, could if they really wished, play to a single figure handicap.

I should stress that this book is not a series of golfing gimmicks. I have not discovered one or two particular secrets of the swing which, when put into practice, will allow everyone to play perfect golf. That simplistic idea has to remain a fool's paradise. The basic thesis of the book is that if a genuine attempt has been made to acquire a swing and this has proved unsuccessful, then one of two factors must be responsible. Either the instruction has been misinterpreted or else one's ability is, in certain respects, limited and preventing the execution of the correct swing. In my view, this latter reason is by far and away the major one and I am convinced there is a way round it by intelligent analysis and appreciation of the situation. If we are able to understand the reasons why the top players play as they do, why it is their swings vary, and why it is the rest of us are having so much difficulty in emulating their feats, then I believe we are well on our way towards improving our skills.

Although this volume is aimed principally at the handicap golfer, I am sure it will also be of interest and value to the teaching professionals and talented amateurs. It will not only tell them why they are such competent performers, it will also explain why it is so difficult for them to pass their skills on to the higher handicap golfers. There is undoubtedly a lot of truth in the old adage which suggests that those with the most ability make the worst teachers, and in this respect I am certain there are many teaching professionals who are at a complete loss as to the real nature of the difficulties that the average club golfer is up against. I will therefore be rewarded indeed if this book is instrumental in putting the art of teaching the golf swing to the handicap golfers just one small step further down the road.

The thought will have crossed many perceptive readers' minds as to why the author is not a golfer of national or international status. Here I am, a handicap golfer, claiming to have an insight into a fundamental secret of the golf swing. I readily admit that my one and only claim to golfing fame is that for one fleeting year I was the amateur Senior Champion of the North-East of Scotland. Very small beer, but perhaps illustrative of how a struggling club golfer can on occasions get his act together. My inherent golfing ability is extremely average, but by the application of theory allied to determination, it is often quite amazing what can be achieved. As a medical doctor I have studied the human body and its frailties, I have also studied the mechanics of the golf swing, and in this book I attempt to weld these two together.

My aim is not to teach the golf swing – that is the job of the professionals. The real point I wish to put over is, by making use of the available knowledge and teachings, to describe, in terms that are relevant to the human body, why we, as struggling club golfers, are finding such difficulty in following through the advice that our professional instructors give to us. Make no mistake, we will not all end up as scratch golfers; that is an impossible goal and most of us must accept from the start that we will always have our limitations. Nevertheless, I am certain most of us will be amazed how much improvement is actually lying latent within us.

In the writing of the book I have tended to use the male gender. I certainly mean no disrespect to the lady golfers (I dare not with my wife being numbered amongst them); it has been done for simplicity and to avoid a constant repetition of "his and her" throughout the text.

At this juncture I would like to take this opportunity to thank my many friends who have assisted me in the preparation of this book. They are too numerous to name individually, but without their help, friendship and criticism, I could not have persisted in this task. They have been stalwarts over the years, they have prompted many ideas, curbed my over-enthusiasm and criticised my many outrageous statements. They have put up with my constant, and I am sure at times very boring conversation. They have done all this and yet have continued to play with me. To Robin, Leslie, Hamish, Alan and the rest of the gang at Deeside Golf Club, I owe them all a great debt of gratitude. Also a special thanks to Colin Farquharson who provided the stimulation needed to change a perpetual personal hobby into the pursuit of publication. Also my thanks to Jill Dick, Ian Hustwick and Harry Greig for their help in the nuts and bolts of putting a book together and on the market.

During the years of writing this book my family have endured greatly. If ever the term "golf widow" had meaning, it must surely be referring to my wife Pat, to Pat and my two sons Angus and Duncan I thank them for the hours they have allowed me to spend on the golf course testing my theories. To my delight, the family have been infected with the golf bug themselves, and while it may be a case of "if you can't beat him, join him", nevertheless, it has been a delight to have enjoyed so many happy family golfing times together and be the proud father of a two times Club Champion, Duncan. My other son, Angus, is the computer buff in the family and without his help I would still be banging away at two-finger typewriter level. I am in total awe at what technology can achieve these days and, again, thank you Angus, for without your pushing me into the realms of modern technology, scanners and word processors, I would never have got this far.

Also my very sincere thanks to John Chillas for writing the foreword to this book. I could not wish to have had it associated with a nicer guy and one who is a great credit to his profession.

Chapter 1

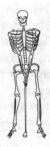

Oh Golf Swing, Wherefore Art Thou?

Why is a powerful and flowing golf swing so difficult for most of us to achieve? Why is it that on the rare occasions when we do alight on a reasonably competent version, it stays for only a fleeting moment in time? Why do we vary so much from day to day, week to week or round to round? Rational thought on the subject would suggest that the golf swing ought to be a reasonably easy movement to perform, the golf ball stays still, the equipment is precision designed, the ground is level for a drive and the ball is even perched on a little peg. Why, in spite of all these advantages does it remain an inescapable fact that the average club golfer hits far more poor shots than he ever hits long and straight?

These questions have intrigued us all but answers to them are by no means easy to find. Good tuition, diligent practice and an understanding of the swing mechanics are regarded as the three principal keys to success. This seems to be sensible enough reasoning, but so rarely does it hold true in practice. Many high handicap golfers do work extremely hard on their swings, they do seek tuition and they do practise intently, but mostly it is to no avail. Often, for a few fleeting moments on the practice ground or on the course, they may feel they are on the verge of discovering the ingredients of a sound, repetitive and grooved swing, the swing that will put them on the fairway off the tee, the swing that will give them precision and accuracy with the irons, the swing that will be repeatable hole after hole, day after day and year after year. Indeed, most of us have felt this quite often, only to find that the elation and euphoria of one minute has plunged into the disaster and despair of the next!

Anyone who has played golf regularly knows how incredibly easy it is for a carefully built-up swing, within seconds, to disintegrate into a primeval, overbalanced and ungainly swipe. On such occasions the gorse bushes creep in, the trees spread their branches, the rough grows and expands as we watch and the formerly expansive fairways shrink into little green strips only inches wide. Our ball, as if sensing the freedom of the occasion, celebrates by sweeping from the turf or tee like an inebriated swallow and heading for the nearest copse or patch of rough.

It is at times like this that most of us take stock of ourselves and analyse our grip, stance, arc of swing, take-away, follow-through, weight transference, K position, Y position, shin post, left arm, right arm, right elbow, heart position, left shoulder, right hip, club face and all the hundreds of features and gimmicks that have been described and taught over the years. On most occasions any improvement is extremely marginal, but suddenly we may be rewarded, and like a Phoenix from the ashes "the swing", or a new and functional variant of it, will emerge and stay with us for a little while.

Such is the pattern of golf for most of us. We flit from one technique to another, always modifying, always searching; just occasionally we are successful and a steady stable swing appears. We appreciate it is not the perfect swing, but at least it affords us consistency for a period and gets us round the course avoiding most disasters. Once we try to improve, as likely as not, we will be back in no-man's land again. On the very few occasions when we do achieve a perfect shot, it seems to come right out of the blue, it just seems to happen, a perfect combination of every part of the body with no strain or effort, one cohesive functioning movement of body and club. Alas, the minute we try and analyse it or repeat it, it vanishes.

Golf literature provides us with very few explanations of this will-o'-the-wisp swing phenomenon. Indeed, one could say, explanations are tactfully avoided as it is not good business to put forward a view that the golf swing is not reproducible in everybody. Many golf professionals take an extremely positive line on this and stoutly maintain that a good golf swing is reproducible in everyone, provided they will follow instructions and provided they will practise diligently. I both agree and disagree. I would agree that a good-looking swing is perfectly achievable by all of us, but a swing that is both classic and powerful is certainly not within the grasp of all of us. I maintain that the possession of a sound swing does not appear to be related to the amount of tuition one receives, nor to one's physical build, nor to any quantifiable assessment of intelligence. This is not to say that practice, tuition, physique and intelligence are not of use. Of course they are. However, there is not as direct a relationship between these assets and the acquisition of a good sound golf swing as many experts would have us believe. We all know of golfers who have practised little, have had virtually no tuition and yet play to low single-figure handicaps with almost monotonous regularity. Nick Faldo only took up the game at the late age of fourteen and yet was winning top amateur awards three or four years later and Ryder Cup honours by the age of twenty. Seve Ballesteros was an established world star by the same age. There has to be more to golfing prowess than can be achieved by tuition and practice alone.

Let us therefore delve somewhat deeper and see if we can discover an answer to this intriguing question of who possesses or does not possess "natural golfing ability", and indeed, just what natural golfing ability really is. Why do some individuals have the ability to swing well almost from the time they first hold a club? Is there an, as yet undiscovered, ingredient that is common to all good golfers, but is missing or lacking in others? If we can find this missing link, can we reproduce it?

These questions have rightly concerned golfers and scientists over the years and much thought and research has been undertaken. It would be invidious to mention any particular golf book and claim it was superior to others, as all undoubtedly have their merits. However, Ben Hogan's contribution, "The Modern Fundamentals of Golf", published in 1957, must remain a landmark in golf writing. His book was then, and has remained, a masterpiece of description. In it Hogan described and illustrated the swing with absolute clarity and meticulous attention to detail. He described and analysed all possible aspects of the swing – the grip, the stance, the backswing, the downswing, the plane of the swing ... in fact just about every position of every muscle and joint in the body. Each and every facet came under his expert scrutiny. His book has remained a classic text on anatomical positional golf tuition and in it Hogan undoubtedly set the path for many others to follow.

Despite his book's magnificent and meticulous attention to detail, I have to say that I do not regard it as a complete work. A vital ingredient is missing and it is this same ingredient that is missing in nearly every other golf book or piece of advice written about the golf swing. Almost without exception they fail in their attempts to tell the reader the complete story of "how" to swing the club and hit the ball. They certainly tell the reader what the correct mechanical movements are supposed to be, but they fail to tell him how to convert this mass of anatomical and mechanical detail into a vital live and active swing movement. They persist in the conviction that accurate positional and anatomical details are the pathway to a perfect swing. I would not disagree that this is a vital part of the answer; however, it is only one part, and the practical evidence of generations of tuition and teaching has shown that this approach to tuition has failed to produce results in the vast majority of golfers. There still remains a missing factor and it is this factor we must know more about.

In recent years, scientists have tried to improve on this rather limited anatomical or mechanical approach to golf tuition. They have investigated the physics of the swing in the hope that an explanation and understanding of the actual mechanics of the swing will provide the pupil with a mental image of the type of movement he is required to produce. In doing this the scientific researchers have taken golf tuition one further step along the road. They have produced fascinating information concerning the action of the arms, wrists and club shaft as being a mechanical flail system. They have emphasised the requirements to turn the shoulders, to cock the wrists and to release at the ball. However, as regards the actual live swing, they still leave the prospective golfer in as much confusion as ever as to how to carry through this mechanical swing movement if it fails to come naturally in the first instance. Their contribution is a more sophisticated explanation of what happens but it still falls short of an explanation of how to make it happen

Many professional teachers are acutely aware of this deficiency and attempt to overcome the problem by stressing particular component parts of the swing. They may use descriptive phrases such as "lead with your left side" or "hit against a braced left side" or "feel as if you are balancing a tray with your right hand at the top of the backswing". These phrases and hundreds more like them using the word "feel" are attempts by the instructor to impart to the pupil the sensations he himself has and which he thinks the pupil ought to have. It is certainly a serious attempt to supply the factor that will link individual movements into an integrated and total movement, but the trouble is they are descriptive and subjective phrases. They are made up from the teacher's own personal experience and as such are not readily communicable to others with any degree of reliability or consistency. This method suffers from the very fact that it is a subjective approach, and only if the pupil is of the same bodily make-up as the teacher will the phrases be totally meaningful. More recently, video techniques have helped in this respect, and the Faldo/Leadbetter tapes demonstrating training techniques such as tucking a towel under the armpits or keeping the club shaft into the belly-button are undoubtedly useful additions to the spoken word. However, they still lack a common thread which will link them to any or all handicap golfers with a swing problem.

I remember the first occasion when I came face to face with this apparent deficiency of professional tuition. I was a raw young student of seventeen years of age and at the time was playing reasonably well to a nine handicap. My swing was functional and repetitive but rather ungainly and I tended to strike the ball with the weight on the back foot. I decided I had little chance to improve without expert help and arranged a series of lessons with my club professional. I went to these lessons buoyed up with enthusiasm and hope. I was prepared to work hard. I expected to be given insight into the perfect swing. To my bitter disappointment, the advice I received was that my swing, grip and set-up was reasonable and I should alter very little. The professional suggested I concentrate all my efforts on trying to get my weight through at impact.

I remember coming away from these few lessons a very dispirited and disappointed young man. The professional had in the end told me little that my friends had not already advised. I knew I hit the ball off the back foot; what I wanted from him was advice on *how* to get the weight over, not just to be told to get it over. I had been trying to do that for myself throughout the previous year with little success. I remember at the time convincing myself, with all the naivety of youth, that golf professionals as a group were undoubtedly in a dastardly plot together and had connived amongst themselves to hide the ultimate secret of the golf swing and prevent the amateur from getting in on it.

Stupid, I know, and with more mature thought I realised what an absurd idea this was. The simple fact was that this particular club professional was a creditable performer on the course, but not of the highest calibre as a teacher of the game. Despite the disappointments of this experience I still retained a sneaking feeling at the back of my mind that somewhere in my immature thoughts there had to be a few grains of truth. That feeling continued to haunt me over the years but whenever I tried to rationalise it further I still could not find complete answers. Why were certain groups able to play better golf than others? Indeed, were professionals actually holding back on something?

It has been said that "man will occasionally stumble over the truth, but most of the time he will pick himself up and continue on". It took me many years before I realised I had in fact stumbled over a truth of sorts in my younger days.

I have now discovered the secret which that professional denied to me all those years ago, the secret that he and most other professionals and top amateurs possess, but fail to pass on. Since discovering this common thread to all golf swings I have found it has added the "why" to the "how" of the golf swing. It has also supplied answers to many other controversies and fundamental questions in golf. For instance, it answers such questions as – What part of the body initiates the swing? Who has potential for top class play and who has not? Should a youngster learn to hit the ball long and hard initially and only turn to control later? Is there one correct golf swing for all of us? Are professionals mistaken when they themselves seek perfection? Why do even the best experts experience slumps of form? One can also hazard opinions as to how the average golf course should be designed and, once designed, what effect alterations would have on the amateur or professional game, which empires would crumble and which would thrive?

Chapter 2

The Secret They Never Tell You

Many years ago on a beautiful balmy June evening, our University golf team, along with our opponents from Birmingham University, were sitting in the distinguished lounge of Royal Liverpool Golf Club. We had just finished a close but victorious match against them and were chatting over the events of the day.

As invariably happens in undergraduate golfing circles, the discussion came round to points of technique of the golf swing, and I well remember an opinion a friend of mine voiced on that occasion. He stated that if anyone did not know instinctively what the correct golf swing was by the age of sixteen or seventeen then he would never become a really low handicap golfer. He amplified this statement by adding that if by that age the golfer was already a category 1 handicap, then tuition should be confined to modifying details of set-up, stance and minor points of technique. The golfer himself ought by that time to have his swing under control.

At the time this struck me as a rather sweeping and almost arrogant statement, one I presumed was brought forth by youthful enthusiasm, perhaps flushed by the success of a recent well-won personal match, or maybe just a swing that was going particularly well for him at the time. However, to my surprise there was a murmur of agreement with his conclusions. For my own part I kept tactfully silent on the subject, for I suspected that any great display of dissent on my part would be likely to put my place in the team in some doubt! Well I appreciated that my place in the team owed as much to the possession of a car as to any particular ability at golf! The truth was that for me, a struggling five handicap player (N.B. I am four shots better now), to assume my swing was instinctive and self-correcting was about as fanciful as a political leader hoping for a one hundred percent vote of confidence.

However, there it was, I had to accept it, a bold statement of fact –
my friend maintained he knew instinctively what the correct swing
should be. Many months later, my place in the team assured, I tackled
him again on the subject. The answer was essentially the same; he
reckoned he knew what the correct swing was, it was something
natural, something he did not have to think about, his body virtually
did it for him. Grip, stance and set-up were something different, on
these he had to concentrate, but the swing itself was a natural
phenomenon ... for him it was just like throwing a stone, opening a
door or climbing stairs. He just didn't have to think overmuch about
position when he took the clubhead back; he, or in fact his body, did
this for him quite naturally. Provided, and he made a great point of this,
he had his hands, feet, shoulders and spine – in fact the whole body –
aligned in a suitable position, then the club was able to go back quite
naturally on the backswing and come through in an arc that assured a
full, accurate, and what is more, a powerful shot. He was able to time
his swing instinctively and direct the power outlet at the point he
desired. However, if his body was not in the correct position at the
outset, or his grip was faulty, the swing itself would function in much
the same way, but the arc and angle at which the clubhead came
through would be such that the ball would not be squarely struck and
a poorly directed shot would result.

Since these early days of student life my friend has produced the
proof of his statements and has for many years been a scratch golfer
and county player. He has achieved these ends, I may add, with far less
practice than me. For me, the swing itself was as much a problem as
the stance, grip and set-up.

Over the years I have read or heard many similar statements by
excellent players and professionals. It seems, for these instinctive
strikers of the ball, the basic swing is a relatively minor problem, for
them it has resolved into a matter of grip, stance, set-up position, short
play, concentration, putting and control of emotion. This is so very
different from the average club golfer; he has all these problems in
abundance but he also has the extra major problem of "the swing"
which these top performers seemingly do not have.

The golf swing is often artificially divided into component parts
such as the backswing, the downswing, the impact area and the follow

through. I want to divide it into only two parts:

1) The muscular component or motor of the swing.
2) The skeletal component or system of levers of the swing.

This simple division makes it quite clear what my friend was talking about. For him, the muscular component (which he called the swing) was a natural and simple movement; the main difficulty in golf for him lay in arranging his skeletal component (i.e. the bones of his skeleton) in such a manner that when his muscular component functioned with its usual smooth and fluid flow of action, it allowed his limbs and trunk (the skeletal component) to move through the correct lever actions which we know and term the classic or correct golf swing. The muscular component is therefore the actual motor of the movement. The skeleton is merely the passive inert framework or system of mechanical levers.

It is quite obvious that as individuals, we possess different capabilities in the efficient control or fluidity of our muscular actions. For example, take the simple skill of walking: we can all walk and we all have much the same training in this basic movement. Despite this, some people walk gracefully and elegantly while others are ungainly and clumsy. Some women will be naturals as fashion models, others will need extensive training. It will be quite possible to teach this group how to place their feet on the ground, how long a stride to take, how to hold their body erect and so on. Their final attempts will never quite reach the same fluidity of action as the natural graceful movers but it would be difficult to distinguish one from the other at the end of training.

Now, if in addition to walking, both were to be asked to run, the natural graceful athlete would cope with this movement instinctively, the other would not. In essence, it is the same movement speeded up but whereas the one could cope the other could not. The point to appreciate is that in some people there resides a natural inborn ability to move correctly – they are fortunate in that they have been born with a muscular motor that is superior to that of their neighbour.

This same reasoning can in turn be translated to the golf swing, and evidence to support such a contention is not hard to find. Over and over again, if we analyse the writings of any of the top professional golfers, we will see that ninety percent of their text will be on subjects such as the grip, set-up, stance, club position at take away, club position at the top of the backswing, club position at impact, club position at follow through – all mechanical information. But try as we might to find out from their writings how they actually achieve these positions as an integrated movement and what do they say? Statements like "just take the club back and hit" or "stay balanced", and then off they go again into a further lengthy anatomical description. One could almost say it's a case of – they know precisely *what* they do, but they know not *how* they actually do it! In other words, their muscular motors are instinctive and carry out the correct muscular actions for them provided that their skeletal component or system of levers is set up correctly at the outset. These talented performers can and do inform us of all the mechanical positions at all stages of their swings, but as yet they do not know how to communicate to us, the struggling golfer, the inner secrets of their muscular motors.

The question is therefore – can the ordinary golfer acquire the gift of a muscular motor that will perform the classic golf swing if he does not already possess it as an inborn gift?

At this early point in the book I would be encouraging and say the answer to this question is a definite yes. Almost every individual ought to be capable of acquiring a satisfactorily functioning muscular motor. However, there will have to be limitations to this and it is unlikely the new acquisition will turn us into a top amateur golfer or even one who will reach the last four of our own club championship. Nevertheless, I believe there is ample scope for a dramatic improvement in all of us.

My approach for the remainder of this book is therefore to describe the mechanics of the golf swing from a skeletal point of view and then use this to build up a picture of the muscular motor that we require in order to operate and activate the correct series of skeletal movements. Only if our muscular motors can be made to perform in a balanced, synchronised and smooth manner will they be able to bring about the movements of the classic golf swing. If they fail to act in this manner then the skeletal component of the body, however well arranged it may be at the outset, will become increasingly disrupted throughout any swing movement.

If we can now go back to my University friend I mentioned at the beginning of the chapter. The truth of his statement is now clear: it was true what he was saying, he himself did possess a near perfect muscular motor, he could therefore instinctively perform a satisfactory swing movement and apart from paying strict attention to his grip and set-up position, he was able to hit repetitive, powerful and classic shots that few of us lesser mortals could match. For myself, with my inferior muscular motor, I was always struggling against him despite any intensive practice that I might undertake. I was completely unable to compete with him in respect of consistently striking the ball long and straight and I had to compensate by doing my best with what I was given in respect of my other inherited skills. I had to make up for my deficiencies in the long game by raising my standards in the short game. As an individual with a high level of hand-eye co-ordination I possessed a pretty fair short game and expertise around the green, but it was up to me to use this to good effect. It meant I was always destined to be the type of player who came from behind, rarely was I ever the master of the situation from the tee. I was a good match player but a poor stroke player.

Because the "natural golfers" possess almost perfect control over their muscular motors, it means they are able to spend much more time and thought on perfecting their skeletal components and paying attention to the positional and anatomical aspects of their set-up. They can think about and envisage the striking of the shot. The less endowed player is in the unfortunate position of having two major variables to contend with, neither of which will provide him with a stable and fixed reference point. He will have a perpetual struggle to find any sort of harmonious match between his muscular and skeletal component, far less envisaging his shot. On the rare occasions when he happens to find a degree of unity between the two components a satisfactory swing may appear for a while; however, it is likely to be a brief and unenduring affair.

Chapter 3

The Gift of the "Naturals"

The conclusion to be drawn from thinking about the muscular component as a single entity is that its most important attribute, if it is to motivate a classic golf swing, is its ability to perform its action as if it were one cohesive unit. In this context, the word ambidextrous springs to mind as it implies the ability to perform movements with equal skill on either side of the body. The concept I have in mind, however, is slightly more than this and implies complete unity of body movement with neither one side nor the other becoming dominant at any stage – in other words, a totality of the whole muscular movement that is synchronised and co-ordinated as a centrally controlled action. There appears to be no word in the English language to express this concept of "totality of body movement" and the nearest I can get to it is to actually coin a new word – "unidextrous". The Latin uni- meaning "having one axis", hence a unidextrous action would mean having a manipulative or muscular skill with only one axis – i.e. a central body axis. In other words, no left or right side dominance, but the muscles working as a single unit. It is this muscular unity, or totality of muscular movement around a central body axis, that powers what we could call the classic golf swing.

We are all born with a certain degree of unidextrous ability, it is not an all or nothing principle and we can all make our bodies function as a single unit if we so wish. However, it is the higher levels of this unified action that are of the greatest importance in the execution of a powerful and accurate golf swing. This is particularly so in the use of the long irons or the driver where length and accuracy are necessary and the urge to use power is instinctive.

Ambidextrous individuals (but for the remainder of this book I will refer to them as unidextrous individuals or unidextrans) have been born with an ability to perform a total or unified bodily muscular movement at or near their top co-ordination levels. A balanced body movement of this degree is denied to the right or left side dominant individual because he or she is incapable of producing a unified body movement at the top power and co-ordination level of their dominant or favoured side. The unidextran, by definition, is therefore the better equipped individual to perform a golf swing at the upper levels of power. Assuming all other things to be equal, this individual will always remain the better performer from tee to green.

Human nature being what it is, it is exceedingly difficult for this talented group of individuals to accept that they are endowed with skills that the majority of their fellow men do not possess. Many of them imagine that because they may use their right hand for everyday functions, they must necessarily be right side dominant. This does not necessarily follow and just because they may not have practised fine finger and hand co-ordinated movements with their left hand, does not mean these skills are not available to the large muscles of the trunk, legs and arms. It is quite feasible for an individual to be potentially and practically unidextrous with his body, arm and leg movements and be a top golfer, and yet at one and the same time not be practised with the fine finger and hand movements of the left hand. Such a person would be convinced he was right side dominant and be totally unaware of the precious gift he possessed of being able, at his upper power levels, to synchronise and unify his body movements as a totality. Many of us fail to develop any unidextrous potential outside sporting pursuits as there is very little need for such a function in our present day right side dominated society.

What then of the unfortunate individuals who are not possessed of unidextrous ability at their top power levels? I am afraid it has to be said that this group (of which I am one) will always remain limited in their ability to perform a unified body movement with anything like the same power and precision as our unidextrous brethren. However, this does not mean we cannot learn to perform unidextrous or balanced movements at a slightly reduced power level, or indeed, learn to adapt to other swing methods.

It is predetermined whether we possess unidextrous skills or not, we have no choice in the matter, our parents decide this fate for us at the outset. If we have any pretensions of reaching the top levels of golf, then it is absolutely essential that we have chosen our parents wisely and that they have endowed us with a muscular component that is possessed of unidextrous qualities at its upper power levels.

The science of inherited potential is exceedingly complex and of no real relevance to this book. However, a simple inheritance pattern of side dominance (Fig.1) might be if one parent was right side dominant, represented by (R.R.) and the other parent was unidextrous, represented by (R.L.). In this example four possibilities exist for the children if we assume they inherit one gene or inheritance factor from each parent.

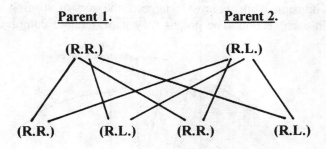

Parent 1.   **Parent 2.**

(R.R.)   **(R.L.)**

(R.R.)   **(R.L.)**   **(R.R.)**   **(R.L.)**

Figure 1. Possible inheritance pattern

In this particular illustration two children would be right side dominant and two would be unidextrous. In other words, there would be a fifty percent chance that each child would be unidextrous. Unfortunately, inheritance is not such a simple matter and parents with blue eyes may have children with brown eyes and vice versa. Such inheritance patterns are termed recessive and may well lie dormant and only emerge a generation or so later. It has generally been accepted that the ratio of dominance of the right side factor over the left is approximately four times and if worked out on this ratio it suggests the percentage of right side dominant individuals in the population may be about 64%, the percentage of left side dominant individuals as some 4% and the unidextrans around 32%. It is my belief that it is around this 32% of the population that all professional and top amateur sport revolves. This group are the "have's" of the sporting world as regards potential for a smooth, powerful, precise and unified muscular movement that incorporates the whole body as one single functioning unit. In essence this was the secret I was searching for at the age of seventeen and failed to stumble over until much later in life. No wonder my club professional was unable to give it to me, only my parents could have done that!

It is clear that the divisions between unidexterity, right and left side dominance are rather arbitrary and they are in no way clear cut or all or nothing divisions. Just because an individual may be right side dominant does not mean he cannot use his left side, there has to be shading within each group and from one group to the next. The pie chart in Figure 2 indicates the likely percentages of the population in each division while Figure 3 suggests the sort of shading of skills within each section. The graphs may appear rather complex at first

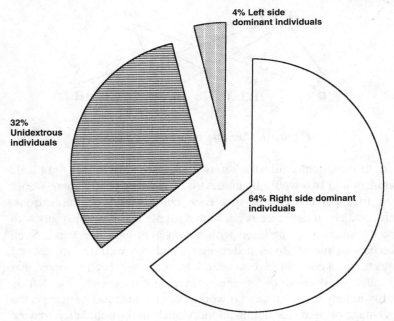

4% Left side dominant individuals

32% Unidextrous individuals

64% Right side dominant individuals

Figure 2. Likely percentage of the population in particular muscular skill areas

sight but they are not really. If each twin column is taken to represent one individual and their left/right side muscular balance, it can be seen that in Figure 3A (the 32% of unidextrans in the population) there are very few individuals within this group who are perfectly unidextrous (I have only depicted one). From this point there will be a gradual imbalance developing, some more dominant right, but a minority to the

Figure 3 A, B Histograms of the likely left/right side muscular balance of the population

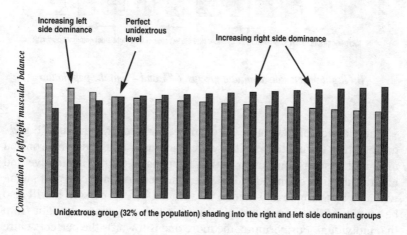

Unidextrous group (32% of the population) shading into the right and left side dominant groups

A. Unidextrous group - 32% of the population

left. However, all this group, despite their gradually increasing muscular discrepancy, have reasonably high unidextrous ability levels and can be considered to be capable of satisfactory unidextrous muscular action.

Figure 3B represents the other 68% of the population with increasingly differential muscular abilities. I have only depicted eleven individuals but they may represent either the sixty-four percent of right side dominant or the four percent of left side dominant individuals in the population. Each group has increasing muscular left or right side imbalance throughout their range.

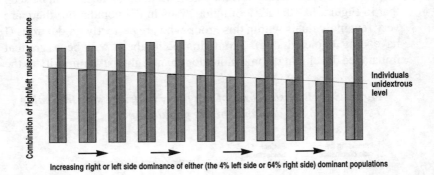

B. Right or left side dominant groups, 64% and 4% of the population

The classic golf swing is a movement that requires the total body's musculature to function as if it were one integrated and synchronised unit, and if such a muscular action happens to be the instinctive and natural function of an individual, then the performance of a golf swing will also be a simple and natural movement for that person. It will also be an action that is unlikely to require much conscious thought from that individual. Furthermore, the more one is towards the perfect centre of balance – i.e. the perfect unidextran – the more instinctive and the more powerful a classic movement will, or can, be. In addition, it will be much easier to maintain and retain that movement when working under adverse conditions such as strong winds or tense competitive situations. The players towards the outer fringes of the unidextrous group (Fig. 3A) are likely to have increasing difficulty in maintaining their swing under adverse conditions.

And so on to the groups represented by 3B, the 68% of left or right side dominant individuals. They are the continuations from the extremes of the unidextrous group and both have inborn in them increasing muscular imbalance. A balanced body movement is not a natural instinct for these individually if they attempt a classic swing, in the first place it will never be a completely natural and instinctive movement for them and they will always be required to exert conscious muscular control over it. In the second place, if any additional stress situation, i.e. adverse weather conditions, or tense match play conditions, is applied to an already achieved swing, it is more than likely that this extra burden will prove to be far more disruptive to these left or right side dominant individuals than it would be to those on the fringes of the unidextrous group.

By my definition therefore, all top class golfers have to be in the broad unidextrous range, and most of the better ones will be likely to be towards the central area of that range. I firmly believe this to be true. Many actually state this in their writings or autobiographies. Sam Snead, the possessor of perhaps the most natural swing ever seen, did not know as a junior whether to play golf right or left handed, neither did Ben Hogan, Johnny Miller or Bob Charles, and David Graham actually changed from left to right. The established young superstar Phil Mickelson is right handed in everything except golf. The new golfing machine and 1997 Masters Champion, Tiger Woods, is undoubtedly perfectly unidextrous in ability and we learn that he actually picked up and swung the club left handed in the first instance. I would suggest his father was fortunate indeed that both he and his wife gave young Tiger the perfect muscular genes, otherwise I would suggest his efforts to create a golfing superstar would have been doomed to failure.

And so it goes on. Rarely can one find a good golfer without above average left side ability if he is right sided and vice versa if he plays left handed. A glance at other sports also supports this view and it is no surprise that similar unidextrous and ambidextrous skills are displayed by cricketers, soccer players and other top sportsmen. Cricket in particular abounds with test and county players who bat right handed and bowl left or vice versa. Far above the average for any population.

Many gifted players, when challenged in respect of their skills, deny they possess instinctive unidextrous action. One top amateur golfer who retained a scratch rating for many years despite little play and virtually no practice disputed he was unidextrous. However, after a little prodding and probing he did admit that he played table tennis left or right handed! One tournament professional I approached with my unidextrous theory also contested it, but on reflection found that he not only buttered his toast with his left hand, but dealt cards with his left hand, filled his pipe, could use a hammer or screwdriver with his left hand. It was a revelation to him to appreciate that a skill he had taken for granted and assumed we all possessed was in fact just not the case. Like most of his colleagues, he believed it was only because he had practised that he was able to achieve a golf swing that was graceful, powerful and balanced. I readily concede to him and to all these other players that it is a gift that can only be developed with practice, but the fact remains that NO AMOUNT OF PRACTICE WILL COMPENSATE FOR THE DEFICIENCY OF AN INBORN SKILL.

How can the rest of us be expected to cope? The short answer has to be – "with difficulty", but having said that, I believe there are ways of overcoming the problem. Essentially we must learn to reduce the power of our dominant right side to match with that of our left side or, failing that, go part of the way along this path and develop a swing technique or set-up that will allow the left side to keep better control of the right side. We will never be able to increase the power and control of our lesser side to match that of our dominant side.

Herein lies the real underlying secret of the golf swing. Difficult though it may be to credit, we must first accept that as mortal men we are of two different breeds: one group amongst us has the built-in potential for a reasonably powerful and balanced golf swing, the other group has not ... the majority, unfortunately, have muscular disharmony in-built. It is possible to compensate for this muscular disharmony, and in certain circumstances it may become almost the equal of the "natural" muscular component. However, it will never be an easy task, the swing will never quite reach the expertise and fluency of the more natural player and it will easily break down under stressful conditions.

One of the unique fascinations of golf is that it is in fact two games in one and while unidextrous skills are a necessity for the long game, they have much more limited application to the short game and this is the reason why a side dominant individual can often excel at this aspect of the game.

At this stage a fairly simple analogy might be helpful to explain the rather complex relationship between the body's muscular and skeletal components. Imagine a twin engined plane with both motors of equal capacity, both capable of functioning at 10,000 revolutions per minute (rpm) and both running as smooth as silk up to that top speed. Imagine that when the two engines are working in tandem they are equivalent to the muscular motors of a Tiger Woods, Nick Faldo, Seve Ballesteros, Ian Woosnam or a Payne Stewart (Fig. 4A) – i.e. capable of perfect unidextrous or unified action.

Figure 4 Analogy of our Muscular Component

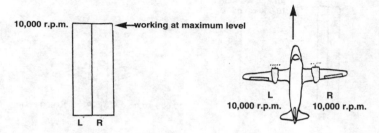

Figure 4A Motor of the top class player

While ambidextrous action would mean that both engines individually were capable of functioning at 10,000 rpm, unidextrous action would mean that both engines were actually running and functioning at equal rpm and were controlled by one throttle lever.

In this aeroplane analogy the skill of co-ordination would be equivalent to the smoothness of the engines, the precision of the bearings, the lack of vibration; top co-ordination would be equivalent to silky smooth running at all speeds right up to the maximum 10,000 rpm. Co-ordination is therefore, not so much how the muscles of the left and right link together (that's unidexterity), it is how smoothly and precisely and accurately each muscular group is able to contract and function and carry out its own skilled movement.

Finally, the muscular build of a person would be equivalent to the capacity of the engines. The bigger the size of the engine the more muscle power would be available.

Now if both engines were of equal capacity and both worked at or near their 10,000 rpm limit and were controlled by one throttle lever, then provided the engines remained smooth and vibration free (i.e. co-ordination remained good) and the flaps, rudder and ailerons etc. were set in a neutral position (i.e. the perfect skeletal set-up position) then the plane would be capable of flying fast and straight (Fig 4A). That's the ideal muscular component or motor of the classic golf swing allied to the perfect set-up, no deviation to the right or left, controlled, powerful and smooth, all the power being produced centrally. The top lady player (Fig 4B) would not have the same capacity as the men, but would be similar in all other respects – i.e. she would have control but not power.

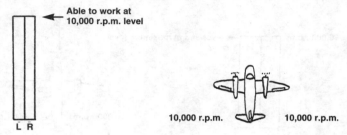

Figure 4B Motor of the top class lady player

Now consider a right side dominant individual (Figs 4C & D). Such an individual would have the same ability as the unidextrous player in the right side engine, but this would not be available in the left engine. On this side the engine would not perform above 8,000 rpm and any attempt to work it above that level would result in it misfiring and losing performance. In other words, with the control by a single throttle lever it would be possible to obtain a smooth unidextrous performance only up to 8,000 rpm. Beyond this point the right side engine would continue to perform up to its 10,000 rpm but the left

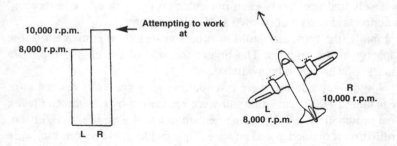

Figure 4C
Right side dominant player trying to work at 10,000 r.p.m. level

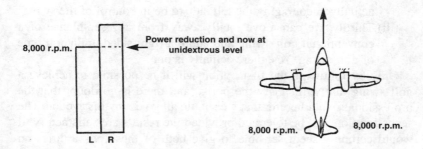

*Figure 4D Same right side player now working at
8,000 r.p.m. level i.e. his unidextrous level*

hand engine would not and could not respond. As a result, if the throttle were pushed past this limit (as we all tend to do), the plane would crab off course. It might be corrected to some extent by alterations to the rudder, flaps or ailerons. In other words, the skeletal set-up could be modified to cope with a degree of muscular imbalance, but it is clear there has to be a limit to the effectiveness of any such compensatory skeletal adjustment. Right side muscular bias above a certain level would therefore not be compensated for by an off-set skeletal set-up. Unfortunately, some sixty-eight percent of us are trapped in this gross muscular imbalance range and it will forever remain our natural instinct to take overall control with our dominant side and move above and beyond the level at which a minor skeletal set-up alteration could compensate.

The logical conclusion would seem to be that those of us who are heavily right side dominant will have to make certain adjustments to our methods if we are to gain accuracy and consistency of shot-making. There are certain options open to us and inevitably we must select one of these to follow.

(i)   We can first of all learn to dampen down the dominant right side musculature until we have achieved unidextrous muscular control. If we can do this we should then be able to follow conventional teaching.

(ii) Secondly, we can move some way along this path of a reduction in right side dominance, but at the same time introduce skeletal modifications to the set-up which will give more assistance in actually encouraging the left side to be in control of the swing.

(iii) Thirdly, we can move totally away from any semblance of a conventional golf swing and adopt a right sided unilateral type of golf swing. Yes, there actually is one!

Only by following the first option will it be possible to achieve a golf swing that will satisfy the purist, and there is no doubt that the professionals would prefer that we should all go down this avenue. The second option will be tolerated provided the results are satisfactory. It would certainly seem sensible to give both of these possibilities an extended trial in the first instance. The third option (which will be looked upon with horror by all professionals) is really only to be tried when all else fails.

In a nutshell, these are the secrets behind the golf swing and perhaps we can now see why it has proved to be such an elusive entity for most of us and why it is likely to remain so as long as our golf instructors persist in limiting their advice to an anatomical or mechanical style of teaching that only fits with a precise and predetermined unidextrous muscular component and ignoring the fact that few of us possess, as a natural instinct, the muscular equipment capable of following through what they are teaching. I feel they will eventually have to become aware that there is a lot more to teaching the golf swing than demonstrating a series of mechanical movements.

Which one of the three pathways a golfer follows is likely to be dictated by the degree of muscular disharmony one inherits. Ambition, dedication and the time one has available are all additional factors. I certainly suggest every golfer should start with lessons from a professional in the conventional manner and initially aim for a conventional swing with a reasonably balanced muscular component. If the dominant muscular side proves too difficult to subdue then I would say – do investigate an alternative pathway and I strongly believe that these alternative pathways should be part and parcel of everyday accepted teaching practice.

Chapter 4

The Skeletal Mechanics of the Ideal Swing

In order to progress with any discussion in depth about the golf swing, unfortunately, it is necessary to be conversant with the basic mechanics of the swing movement. I therefore apologise to the reader for what they may feel is a rather dull chapter. However, I hope the benefits of it will become clearer when I move on to the later chapters.

The inert mechanical, or what I have called the skeletal, component of the golf swing, is composed of two parts. The body, skeleton and legs are one part, the other part is the group of bones that make up the shoulders and arms, and these together with the golf club make up the second part (Figs 5 & 7 Colour Insert). Each of these two distinct skeletal or mechanical units has its own individual identity, its own role to play, and in addition, it must integrate and work in harmony with the other. However, they can be analysed separately.

1st Skeletal Component – The Body and Leg Skeletal Component (Fig 5)

This is the group of bones coloured in red and is made up of the bones and joints of the spine extending from the base of the skull to the tip of the coccyx. It also includes the head, the thoracic cage (chest), the pelvis and the legs. Only two mechanical actions are required of this one unit. The first is that it must provide a stable and erect platform from which the arms and the club (i.e. the second mechanical unit coloured in black) can suspend and act from. The second action is to be active within itself and bring about a corkscrew rotary movement extending from the upper neck, down the spine, body and legs, down to the feet.

The mechanics of this rotary movement require that the upper part of the chest is turned some 80 to 90 degrees relative to the feet with the upper back being directed towards the hole. This turning movement is then graded down the spine with the pelvic area turning some 45 degrees and so on down the hips and knee joints and down to the relatively stable fixtures of the feet on the ground (Fig 6). Slight pulling up (not active lifting) of the left heel is permitted at the end of the backswing but excessive flexing of the left knee is not. It is extremely important that no one part of the body or leg skeleton undertakes an excessive movement in relationship to the rest.

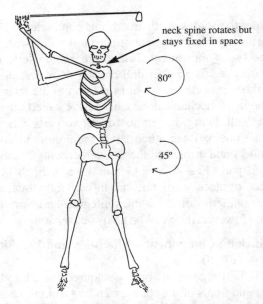

neck spine rotates but stays fixed in space

80°

45°

Figure 6 Rotational movement of the chest, body and legs on the backswing - 80 degrees shoulder, 45 degrees hips

These two mechanical actions of (a) rotation and (b) vertical stability can only be achieved provided the neck portion of the spine is retained at a fixed point in space. It must not move to any great extent either laterally or vertically as it is by this means that the arms and the club (i.e. the second unit) is provided with the stable base which it requires. It is from this stability that the repetitive nature of the golf swing is achieved. One remembers reading how Jack Grout used to grasp young Jack Nicklaus's hair while he swung the club. This was Grout's method of ensuring his pupil's vertical and lateral stability was retained while his upper body rotated.

On the downswing precisely the reverse skeletal movements must take place. The lower part of the unit must initiate the returning rotation and this will unwind back up the legs, pelvis and spine until the upper chest has turned back to its original address position at the point of impact. From this point on, further leg and body rotation will automatically occur and continue on into the follow through position. The important point is that vertical stability is maintained throughout the rotational movement.

2nd Skeletal Component – The Shoulder, Arm and Club Skeletal and Mechanical Component (Fig 7)

The second mechanical unit is made up of part skeleton and part golf club. The skeletal component consists of the two flat plate-like shoulder blades, the two collar bones, the two arms and the hands (Fig 7 Colour Insert). The non-bony element of this mechanical complex is the golf club. It is essential that these two elements of bones plus club combine to form ONE mechanically functional unit.

The sole purpose of this mechanical unit is to allow the club-head to hit the ball at the maximum speed consistent with accuracy and the ability to be repetitive.

The type of mechanical action that is required of this combined bone plus club unit is known as the "FLAIL ACTION". The principle of the flail is quite simple and may be considered as being made up of two rods linked together by a flexible hinge (Fig 8). Such an implement was used by the Ancient Egyptians (and in UK even up to the early 20th century) for threshing corn. The first rod (1) is held in the hands and swept down towards the corn. The second rod (2), which is hinged loosely to it by a leather thong, follows at much the same pace initially, hence the angle between the two rods remains much the same at first (Fig 8 A, B & C). However, if both rods are to reach the horizontal position at the same time, it is necessary for the periphery of the second rod, somewhere along the arc, to start travelling very much faster than the first rod. It is possible to hold this acceleration back

Figure 8 Principle of the two rod flail action

towards the end of the movement with the result that the periphery of the second rod is whipped through the final few degrees of the movement at an ever increasing speed and this is achieved by virtually "throwing away" the second rod and generating speed by the development of centrifugal force (Figs 8 C D & E).

If any of us were given a simple two rod flail system to experiment with, we would find little difficulty in achieving a satisfactory flail action. We would find we were capable of whipping the second rod in at the last second and, the more whip or flail we could achieve towards the end of the movement, the greater would be the speed at the periphery of the second rod. If, however, we were inefficient in our whipping action and let the angle between the two rods open up towards a straight line at the start of the movement then we would have destroyed or "used up" the centrifugal force or whipping action too early in the sequence and might accomplish the task rather better with a single straight rod. The point where the two rods come into alignment is the point of maximum speed and it is therefore the ideal impact area between the clubhead and the ball.

Unfortunately for us, our flail system is not a simple two rod system. Our 1st rod mechanism is our rather complex skeletal structure consisting of our two shoulder blades, two collar bones and two arms. We have therefore been given a triangular shaped 1st rod structure which must act as if it were a single simple rod (Figs 7 & 9). Our 2nd rod is straightforward enough, it is the golf club. The additional complication for us is that the hinge between our two rods, unlike the primitive flail, is capable of initiating muscular action in its own right. It is easy to appreciate that if either the integrity of the triangular shaped 1st rod becomes disrupted, or the wrists initiate their action at the wrong time in the swing sequence, then the correct flail action (i.e. the golf swing) is unlikely to take place.

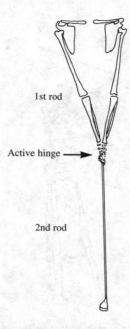

1st rod

Active hinge ───▶

2nd rod

***Figure 9   The first and second rod mechanisms of the flail,
wholly active unit of the skeleton***

Figure 10 illustrates the flail action we have to reproduce, with the active areas being the shoulders and the wrists. The manner by which our triangular shaped 1st rod is able to retain its integrity and is able to function as if it were a simple single rod is by the maintenance throughout the swing movement of three mechanical constants within that first rod triangle (Fig 11 Colour Insert). The first of these three constants is that of the two shoulder-blades and the collar bones which make up the base of the triangle (represented in green) – they must retain a fixed separation distance as they rotate round with the upper body unit. The second constant (red) is the length of the 1st rod and it must be maintained – certainly at address and at impact. The third constant (black) is that the grip must remain intact, uniting the two arms of the rod throughout the swing. In the first illustration equal muscular tension in both arms is maintaining the constant height of the triangle rather than relying on a fixed and rigid skeletal unit. In the

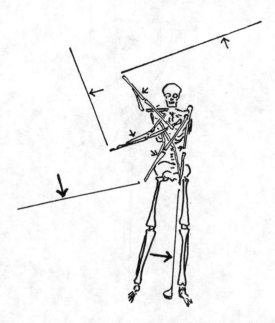

Figure 10 The skeletal flail action active at the shoulders and wrists

second illustration it is the straight and rigid left arm that is acting as the height maintainer.

Provided that the first two of these mechanical constants, the width of the base and the height of the triangle, are maintained throughout the swing then the third constant – the grip – is also likely to remain intact and carry out its function as a hinge, albeit, a hinge that has an active muscular element incorporated in it. While the ideal situation is that all three constants should remain intact throughout the whole swing movement, the integrity of the base has to be the most important. If it breaks, then the grip MUST also fail (piccolo grip).

The maintenance of the length of the 1st rod is not quite so crucial in all circumstances. In the Y set-up (Figs 12,14A & first illustration in Fig 11) it is possible for the left elbow to break, to a minor degree, on the backswing, but provided the height of the rod is reformed to its original length at impact all will be well. In this respect, the immortal Harry Vardon had an extremely bent left elbow at the top of his backswing and many modern golfers, for example Nick Faldo, is by no means totally rigid at his left elbow throughout his swing. The crucial point is therefore that while the constancy of the base of the triangle and the integrity of the grip are mandatory requirements, there is not

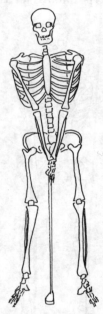

Figure 12 The Y set-up, or skeletal basis for the "Theoretically Ideal" swing. This set up requires to be matched with a perfect unidextrous muscular component

so rigid a requirement as regards the height of the rod throughout the swing, and provided the original length of the rod is reproduced at impact the left elbow may bend slightly on the backswing. The constancy of length of the 1st rod throughout the swing is normally achieved by either the left arm being kept straight throughout the whole swing sequence (this pertains in the Reverse K set-up – Figs 13, 9, 14B & second illustration of Fig 11), or by, in the Y set-up (Fig 14A) the muscles acting across both elbows at a fairly even tension. In this situation the elbows may flex on the backswing but the height of the rod is maintained by the equal muscle tension and is reproduced back at impact.

Figures 14 A and B (Colour Insert) show the swings in diagrammatic form and in each case the three constants are maintained at address, throughout the swing, and at impact. Impact would be a reproduction of the address position as far as the flail unit is concerned.

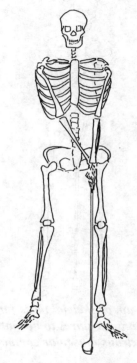

Figure 13
***The reverse K set-up - requires a slightly dominant left side
muscular component***

These drawings are much the same as Figure 11 but, as an addition, the link to the body may be imagined as if it were a coat-hanger with the hook hitched round the neck spine. If the two arms of the coat-hanger (i.e. the base of the 1st rod of the triangle) remain straight and do not fold, and the left arm (or both elbows with even tension) keep the length of the 1st rod intact, then the grip is also likely to remain intact and the integrity of the triangular rod will be maintained throughout the swing. If this happens then a repetitive flail action is likely to be achieved. In the Y set-up swing (Fig 14A), the shape of the triangular 1st rod of the flail will be that of an isosceles triangle at address and impact. In the Reverse K set-up (Fig 14B), it is the left arm that maintains the height of the 1st rod, and the triangle will be a right angled triangle at both address and impact positions.

The Link Mechanism and the Integration of the Two Mechanical Units (Fig 15 Colour Insert)

If the two separate skeletal or mechanical units are to combine and produce a single and fluid backswing and downswing movement, then it is clear that the continuity of this action must take place through the area of their common link. This link happens to be the connection between the base of the flail unit – i.e. the shoulder blades and collar bones, and that of the upper part of the chest or thorax. This mechanical connection therefore has to function efficiently and effectively if there is to be any transfer of mechanical movement from the base of the flail onto the body and down the legs on the backswing and in the reverse direction on the downswing

Without going into too much anatomical detail, the essential requirement for this vital connection to function efficiently is that the two shoulder blade base of the flail unit (i.e. the coat hanger) must rotate round some 80 to 90 degrees at the top of the backswing. However, only some 10 degrees of this turn is achieved by independent mechanical movement of the base of the flail unit relative to the chest wall (Fig 15). The vast majority of the turn must be achieved by the whole upper chest turning – i.e. we are now talking about the necessity for the whole upper body and chest to rotate and carry round with it the base of the 1st rod, or flail unit.

It must be appreciated at this early stage that to hinge the shoulder joints alone – i.e. where the upper arms are set into the shoulder sockets (Fig 16 Colour Insert), is NOT effective turning of the base of the flail. Of course these joints must hinge, but not in place of upper body turning. If shoulder joint hinging is the only, or the predominant movement carried out, then there is little or no mechanical movement being passed on to the body and leg unit, and to all intents and purposes the two skeletal units will remain as independent units. Rotation of the upper body is required to link the body to the arm movement, but it must be remembered that this body rotation must also be relative to the feet remaining related to the ground. One notices that Justin Leonard practises this initial movement prior to his full swing. I suggest he is making sure that the two shoulder/left arm right angle of his 1st rod remains constant for his initial 10° or so of movement. This ensures he doesn't hinge the shoulder joints too early and miss out on a full body turn.

Figure 16 illustrates the faulty movement in that the club has reached much the same position on the backswing as in Figs 14 A & B but it has been achieved the easy way by breaking the left elbow excessively and hinging the shoulder joints and no doubt breaking the grip. Note that the base has only turned about half the amount it should have. In other words, movement has not been transferred onto the body unit and it will not be able to transfer power back to the flail unit on the downswing.

In summary, we can therefore say that the full mechanical movements of the skeleton on the backswing are –

1. A flail angle must be created between the 1st and 2nd rods.

2. That the base of the flail must remain a constant width.

3. That there is maintenance of the length of the 1st rod.

4. That there is a full 80 to 90 degree turn of the base of the flail unit.

5. That the grip remains intact.

6. That finally, there is a graded rotation of the body from the neck to the ground while at the same time, the vertical height is maintained.

If all these mechanical or skeletal actions occur correctly, then there will be a smooth flow of mechanical movement from the club head to the feet, the flail angle will be primed, the body will be rotated, but it will also remain vertically and horizontally stable and finally, the whole movement ought to be capable of repetition.

In the downswing the mechanical movement must start from the lower part of the body – principally, the left leg or left hip, the pelvis will unwind and the mechanical movement will then work up the spine and rotate the upper chest back to its original position. With this de-rotation must automatically come round the two shoulder blade base of the 1st rod of the flail, and this returning movement will trigger off the flail action, with the 1st and 2nd rods coming into alignment at the point of impact. The whole mechanical movement, if correctly carried out, will continue automatically on into the follow through.

This is the complete mechanical role that the skeleton and the golf club play in the golf swing, and a reasonably close analogy of these skeletal mechanics would be to imagine the legs and spinal unit as if it were a sort of gallows post with the horizontal part of the gallows being the neck spine. The head would be stuck on the end of the horizontal arm by a very flexible universal joint. One should look on the base of the flail unit as being a coat-hanger with the hook of the hanger hitched over the neck spine but only free to move through some 10 or so degrees before being limited by hinged links (i.e. the collar bones) to the gallows post (Fig 17 Colour Insert). It can be seen that any turning of the coat-hanger (i.e. the shoulder blade, collar bone base of the 1st rod) beyond a limiting 10 degrees requires that the upper part of the vertical gallows post and the horizontal arm itself be rotated. This rotation is then graded from the top to the bottom until the desired additional 80 degrees of upper body turn is accomplished (Fig 18 Colour Insert). The lower end of the post must remain fixed to the ground.

Note that the horizontal part of the gallows post (i.e. the neck) has turned within itself but has not moved in space, it has stayed in precisely the same vertical and horizontal position throughout the swing movement and has supported and suspended the coat-hanger with the arms at its extremities. Keeping the head still has always been a well known axiom in golf, but to my mind there are dangers of blind adherence to such advice. Certainly, the neck spine must remain stationary in space, but at the same time it must not be impeded in its rotational movement, as it is this rotation that allows the upper chest to turn and transmit the movement from the base of the flail on down the body on the backswing, and vice versa on the downswing. Stability of the neck (and therefore the head) will provide the consistency and repetitive nature to the swing, but neck stability without rotation is destructive.

One or two additional points in this analogy are worth noting. The turning of the body and leg complex has to be a movement which is graded from the top to the bottom (Fig 18) with no one part of the spine or legs taking an excessive role. As we will see in the next chapter, this is necessary in order to stretch the muscles of the trunk and legs in an even fashion and prepare them for their recoil action. To turn the whole gallows post round might achieve much the same effect at chest level but to do this would not stretch and activate the body and leg musculature. In addition, a point I mentioned earlier, to flex the shoulder joints alone (Fig 16) i.e. where the arms are set into the shoulder blades, would be to fail to turn the base of the flail unit the coat-hanger itself must be turned in order to activate the link with the body and this can only be done by turning the upper body. Not to do this would be to leave all the movement within the flail unit and ignore the essential power unit of the body.

Most golf tuition follows very much the pattern of what I have been saying, but obviously with a lot of embellishments regarding swing planes etc. But the point I want to stress is that while it is our bones that carry out these mechanical movement for us, it is not our bones which initiate them or in any way control these movements. It is the job of our muscles to do this for us. We therefore have to know about our muscular component and how it does or does not function if we are to bring about the mechanical movements we have just seen. I do not say there is anything seriously wrong with mechanical teaching, but it is important to appreciate that mechanical tuition is only one part of the story and very often fails to achieve the desired result. In these situations (i.e. a large percentage of the golfing population) I believe the role of the muscular component must be explored and explained as, at the end of the day, it is the muscles that will determine how effective the golf swing mechanics will be.

Close analysis of all the movements of the Y set-up swing that I have described in this chapter shows that they have all occurred around a central axis. The rotation of the base of the flail unit is from a mid-line coat-hanger hook hitched over a centralised neck spine. The gallows supportive action is centralised in its action. The two arms have functioned as if they were one. The grip is a unified central action. The rotation of the neck spine and chest is central in its action. It really does begin to look as though only a unidextrous muscular action could possibly be expected to motivate and activate the inert and passive skeletal system of this set-up and allow it to undertake the movements of what I will from now on call, not the Y set-up swing, but the "Theoretically Ideal" golf swing, as it is the natural swing of the perfect unidextran and can therefore be taken as the basic or centralised swing concept from which all other swings are varients. In other words, it is the reference point from which all other swings may be compared.

Chapter 5

The Muscular Mechanics of the Ideal Swing

"The music is not in the notes" is an often quoted phrase to distinguish between a technically perfect and professional performance as compared to a recital that has transcended this to a level that brings out all the emotion and flavour that a composer intended. If much the same sentiment were to be directed at the golf swing it would not be unfair to suggest that an apt phrase might be – "the swing is not in the mechanics". This could perhaps be amplified by the further statement that – "it is to be found in the mind and the muscles". Indeed, it is muscles that breath life into our inert skeletal systems and produce the swings that are such a joy to watch and a pleasure to enact. It is therefore to muscles and their controlling mechanisms that we must look if we are to provide the answers to our golf swing problems.

If we look at our body's muscular component in more detail we will find that not one muscle extends across the mid-line, we are all made up of two mirror image systems that have to work in perfect tandem (i.e. unidextrous movement) if the muscular complex as a whole is to achieve the sort of balanced and repetitive skeletal movements we now know as the *"theoretically ideal"* or classic golf swing.

To achieve this balanced muscular and skeletal movement we possess three vital links across our two muscular halves. Two of these links are mechanical, while the third is neurological. The two mechanical links are firstly, the ground between our feet, and the second is the spine and the other centrally related bony structures of the chest. The third link, the neurological one, is the brain with its communicating system of peripheral nerves. It is this vital link that will ultimately determine the use that we as individuals make of our mechanical or skeletal component. The genetically balanced individuals amongst us are quite obviously off to a head start in this respect.

Basic physiology of muscle suggests it is capable of doing two things. It is capable of either being lengthened or stretched (provided it is initially relaxed). On the other hand, it is capable of being contracted or shortened (provided it is initially lengthened). It is impossible for a muscle to carry out both these functions at one and the same time. In addition, it is by reciprocal action of muscles acting across joints that controlled movements of joints take place. If any one muscle contracts and remains in a contracted state when it should be relaxed and lengthened, or it relaxes when it should be contracted and shortened, then movement of the associated joint will be restricted or ineffective.

In order to undertake a precisely controlled total body movement such as the golf swing, it is necessary that not only must reciprocal action take place across any single joint, it must also take place across the mid-line of the body and up and down the length of the body. It is at this point that the majority of us will find our greatest difficulty as we now know approximately 68% of us are born defective in our bilateral or across body, muscular control – particularly as we inch towards the upper levels of power. I will come back to this point later as it is the basic cause of most of our golfing troubles, but for the moment, it is important to know a little bit more about how our muscular component brings about the mechanical movements of the classic or theoretically ideal golf swingwe saw in the last chapter.

[At this stage of the book I appreciate that the text is beginning to become rather technical and somewhat boring for the average reader. I therefore suggest missing out the rest of this chapter and jumping on to Chapter 5A where I have given a short synopsis of the essential information regarding the muscular component].

The muscles which perform the mechanical movements of the golf swing can be looked upon as being arranged into **three** distinct groups. Three groups, but with an anatomical continuity between them so that a continuous flow of muscular movement is possible from one group to the next. While each of the three groups is obviously important, the central or middle one, must take pride of place as it is this group that not only links the two skeletal units together, it also acts as the bond between the other two muscular groups. It is this muscular unit that links the whole swing action as one cohesive movement.

The muscles of this central or linking group can be regarded as being arranged in the form of a ring or collar of four muscles around the upper chest and back of the neck (Fig 19 Colour Insert). In this position this ring acts as the active muscular motor between the two skeletal units of the body and the flail; it acts between the base of the flail unit and the upper part of the body and only if the four muscles of this ring perform their tasks efficiently (and unidextrously) will it be possible for the correct skeletal or mechanical action to be transferred from one skeletal unit to the other. If the four ring muscles fail to co-ordinate their actions, then not only will the base of the flail unit become disrupted (and along with it, the whole 1st rod of the flail, and that means disaster), but any flow of movement from the arms to the body and vice versa will be inhibited and the two mechanical units of the arms and the body will not work in harmony.

The other two muscular groups (of the three) are integral to the two main skeletal units – i.e. the body and legs skeletal unit and the flail unit, however, they are connected to each other through the medium of the ring of four muscles which is common to both skeletal units. The body and leg musculature descends from the shoulder ring as a circular sheath around the body and then on in a longitudinal fashion down the legs (Fig 20A & B Colour Insert), while the muscles of the flail unit also extend from the ring in the other direction, but act across the shoulders, elbows and wrists (Fig 21 Colour Insert).

For the skeletal movements of the *"Theoretically Ideal"* golf swing to take place it is necessary that each of the three muscular groups acts in perfect harmony, within themselves, across their mid-lines and in sequence with their adjacent group. If any muscular group fails to act correctly within itself, or fails to work in harmony with the next group, then the skeletal mechanics of the classic swing simply cannot and will not take place (however much anatomical tuition may be given!). There is nothing the skeletal units or bones can do to rectify this, even though the ideal Y set-up may have been achieved at the outset. Ideal action can only take place provided ideal muscular balance – and action – is achieved at the outset, **and is maintained throughout the swing.**

The Action of the Muscular Ring – The Muscular Link Between the Two Skeletal Units

I have suggested that the ring of muscles around the upper chest and neck may be regarded as if it were a ring made up of four separate muscles. In actual fact it is four groups of muscles with widely diverse functions. However, little is to be gained by becoming too complex and it is convenient to regard it as if it were actually made up of a simple ring of four individual muscles and I call this ring the "Trapezius/ Pectoral ring" (Fig 19). Two Trapezius muscles are stretched across the upper back and base of the neck while two Pectoral muscles are stretched across the upper front of the chest. One end of each of these four muscles (or muscle groups) is attached to the base of the flail unit (via the shoulder blades or upper arm), while the other ends are attached to the skeletal body unit (either the mid-line of the chest at the front or the mid-line of the neck and thoracic spine at the back). By means of these skeletal attachments, these four muscles are able to act as the active motivators of the mechanical link between the two skeletal units (remember there are only two skeletal units, but three muscular groups).

If two opposing muscles of the ring are relaxed, and because of their relaxation, are lengthened; and the other two opposing muscles are contracted and because of this, are shortened, then it means the bony fixtures at the ends of these muscles must move round. Hence, if two opposing muscles of the ring, for example the left Pectoral and the right Trapezius group (Fig 22 Colour Insert) contract and shorten (green) while the other two relax and permit themselves to be lengthened (red), then the two shoulder blades (i.e. the constant width base of the flail unit) must move a certain amount round the chest wall. This is precisely what happens, and must happen, to initiate the golf swing (Figs 15 & 22). It is by this muscular means that the base of the flail unit is turned relative to the body for its initial few degrees of turn and then, with these and many other more powerful chest and back muscles coming into play, the base of the flail is carried on round, along with the whole upper body, for a further 75 to 80 degrees, thus completing some 90 degrees of turn. While all this is being achieved, the base of the flail unit has (or should have) retained its constant width.

This base of the flail and the upper body turning can only be maximised provided that the left Trapezius muscle (that is the muscle group from the left shoulder blade across the back to the base of the neck); and the right Pectoral muscle group at the front (red) i.e. the reciprocal muscles that have to relax, do RELAX completely and allowed themselves to be ELONGATED and passively lengthened (Fig 22). If they do not do this, then full and effective upper body turning cannot and will not take place. These two relaxed and stretched muscles of the ring (and the other body, trunk and leg muscles) will in their turn eventually become the active contracting muscles of the downswing and it will be the turn of the right Trapezius and left Pectoral muscles etc. to relax and be passively lengthened. If any one, or combination of these four groups of muscles, does not relax or contract when they should, then the muscular ring will not work and it will be impossible for the correct skeletal or mechanical movements to be passed on from the base of the flail unit on to the body.

I have laboured at some length about the action of the shoulder ring of muscles, but I believe it is absolutely fundamental to the correct action of the golf swing, and without this initial action being 100% correct the rest of the swing mechanics must inevitably fail. Remember, the shoulder muscles are the only linking mechanism that we possess between the arms and the body and it must function correctly. The concept I have described of RELAXATION and passive LENGTHENING or stretching of a muscle in order to prime it for subsequent contraction is something that, to the best of my knowledge, has never been highlighted in any previous book on golf. I suggest the reader thinks deeply about it at this stage particularly of the left Trapezius muscle as it really is the most crucial aspect of the golf swing and so few handicap golfers get this initial muscular action correct.

The important point to appreciate is that only relaxed muscles will be capable of being stretched and only stretched muscles will give a good powerful contraction. Relaxed muscles (but the correct ones) must therefore be a requirement for the backswing and it is for this reason that any generalised muscular tension around the shoulders is so dangerous. I suggest the reader tries it out on himself and completely relaxes around the shoulders while in the address position and then attempts to even further relax and EXTEND and

LENGTHEN the muscle on the left side of the neck between the left shoulder socket and the neck spine (the left Trapezius group). Do the same to the Pectoral group that extend from the mid-line at the front of the chest to the right shoulder socket. (This latter movement is perhaps the most difficult for the right side dominant individual to undertake, and omission of it creates the classic flying right elbow, whereas activation of it brings the right shoulder almost straight behind the neck with the right elbow pointing down).

Note that it really does not require any great effort to accomplish lengthening of the correct muscles and at the same time bringing about a good shoulder turn. Provided the whole group of muscles are relaxed initially, then shoulder ring turning is easy and this relaxed turning – almost without conscious thought – has continued down the body in a spiral down to the firm base of the feet on the ground.

It is also worth reminding ourselves that it is our own reciprocal contracting muscles that achieve this muscular lengthening and passive stretching for us, and we should appreciate that we are not trying to work with these muscles in the way we would to move boulders or heave ton weights about. Ninety five percent of us really have little or no conception of the minimal amount of muscular effort that is required to achieve effective lengthening of the reciprocal muscles and at the same time produce a full and productive shoulder turn.

Relaxed muscular lengthening is the reason why the better golfers appear so effortless in their swing movements and hit the ball so far. It is because they are using muscles that have little or no tension in them that makes them stretch further and provide a more powerful downswing contraction. The majority of us try to achieve these same ends with muscles that are far too tense or unbalanced and all we achieve with such an aggressive or tension loaded approach is to severely limit the amount of mechanical movement that is possible and to fail to prime and lengthen the muscles for their subsequent contraction. Bob Murphy, the American Senior golfer, is perhaps the best example that I am aware of, of a golfer who displays everything that a relaxed shoulder turn backswing ought to be – he really is a superb example.

So I would say, remember that it must be a conscious relaxation of the muscles of the ring that must be the key thought for the backswing – especially the left shoulder to neck group. I like the thought of

droopy shoulders at the address position. (Many cricketers have even got over the problem of the backswing by starting their swing from the top – try it sometime for the golf swing and feel the power and improvement in balance).

The Action of the Muscles of the Flail Unit

If the muscles of the ring have acted correctly and have achieved their dual purpose of both turning and keeping intact the base of the flail unit, then along with this turning must come round the two arms and the club. The initial few degrees of this backswing movement will result in only a slight alteration of the arm and club relationship with some rotation and cocking of the wrists and some folding in of the right elbow but little change in the coat-hanger/left arm relationship (Fig 22). As the upper body turn progresses, however, more and more change must take place within the triangular shaped 1st rod if it is to retain its integrity and continue to act as if it were a simple single rod.

If the Y set-up, or *"Theoretically Ideal"* swing, has been adopted, then the height of the 1st rod will be maintained by the tension of the muscles acting across both elbows. This is not a problem provided the width of the base of the flail remains constant (Fig 14A). Much the same will also apply to the grip, and it also will be easy to maintain intact provided that both the base of the 1st rod and the height of the rod remain constant during the backswing. If, however, the base of the rod breaks (i.e. poor muscular ring function), then neither the height of the rod nor the firm grip can be maintained and the integrity of the whole 1st rod will break up, and with it the whole swing (Fig 30A & B).

The only additional muscular action necessary in the flail unit on the backswing is to develop the flail angle between the 1st and second rods – i.e. the wrist angle between the arms and the club. The angle developed is crucial and obviously this will depend on the grip. This is the realm of the experts.

The Action of the Muscles of the Body and Legs

The Trapezius/Pectoral ring of muscles is, as we have learnt, not only an integral part of the base of the flail unit, it is also the upper part of the tube-like muscular sheath that extends down the body and continues on longitudinally down the thighs and legs (Fig 20).

Effective use of this muscular tube requires that its action be perfectly unidextrous and balanced with reciprocal muscles relaxing and being lengthened and elongated while others are contracting and bringing about the turning movement. This movement must be from the top to the bottom with the aim being to bring about a centralised corkscrew rotary movement of the body and legs in an even and clockwise fashion from the shoulders to the feet. There must be no break in this passive muscular lengthening process from the top to the bottom. An excessively flexed left knee would be sufficient to break this muscular chain and while such an action may well achieve an upper body turn of some 90 degrees, it would be a mechanical upper body turn that was without productive muscular elongation and stretching down the body. If this is done then any power start for the downswing from the lower body would be impossible – in other words, muscles would not have been stretched and lengthened. To lengthen muscles both feet must stay in contact with the ground – not in a leaden, rigid or fixed way, but in what might be described as an active, muscular balanced contact.

Figures 20A & B illustrate the action of the body and leg muscles on the backswing with the tube winding round from the top in the direction of the arrows. On the downswing the tube unwinds from the bottom upwards in the direction of the arrows.

It would seem to me that the peculiar practice swing movement that Corey Pavin undertakes before each and every shot is in fact his way of giving a test run to himself of each of his three muscular elements. It is rather like a mini version of the unfolded swing illustrated in Figure 28, but is sufficient to give him a muscular memory of the required shot.

The Vertical Support Muscles

There is a fourth group of muscles that so far I have omitted to mention. These muscles are an integral part of the body group and carry out the important, but rather less dramatic, role of maintaining the erect nature of the spine. These muscles are arranged longitudinally up and down the spine and, along with the leg muscles, are responsible for maintaining the vertical posture which is so essential if the flail unit is to suspend and rotate freely from the upper chest and neck spine. It is this vertical support that allows the flail to maintain its repetitive action (Fig 23 Colour Insert). In carrying out their task of vertical support these longitudinal muscles must not become so rigid that they impede the action of the ring and its rotational ability, nor must they become excessively floppy and allow the neck spine to droop (Fig 24 Colour Insert) and so cramp the essential flailing action of the arms and club unit. These vertical muscles are greatly assisted in their task if the spine is set in the correct position prior to the start of the swing and this requires the pelvis being tilted slightly forward – i.e. the sitting on the bar stool position. A good way of thinking of it is to sit on the bar stool but yet feel tall between the shoulders. Excessively bent knees or too rigid knees will also destroy correct spinal posture (Figs 25 A & B Colour Insert).

The Action of the Downswing Muscles

If the muscular action of the backswing has been performed correctly and the ring, the tube, and the wrists have all undergone unidextrous passive muscular lengthening of the correct muscles, then there ought to be a chain or line of muscles relaxed, elongated (stretched if you prefer the term) extending from the legs, up through the body, across the shoulders and so onto the wrists. One should be aware and feel this chain or line of ready to contract muscles as just waiting for the signal to start their contraction and become the active muscles of the downswing. It is important when they do contract that they do so in the form of a chain reaction that starts from the lower body, works its way up the body, across the shoulders and finally across the wrist muscles. No other sequence than this can be accepted.

If all goes well, there ought to be a gradual acceleration of movement from the lower body, through the shoulder ring, into the 1st rod of the flail unit and finally across the wrists as the club face is flailed or whipped in at the end of the movement. The centrifugal force that is generated by the flail action should take the club and the body on and into the follow through. It is absolutely essential that the three muscular groups contract in this set sequence. If they fail to do this then any summation effect will be destroyed and this will be reflected in a reduction of club-head speed and/or an inaccuracy in striking.

The backswing, on the other hand, does not required any such rigid sequence of muscular events, and in fact, a variety of possibilities is available. Common sense would seem to dictate that a balanced action of the four groups of muscles of the shoulder ring is perhaps the easiest place to start the golf swing as it is the common denominator between the two skeletal units. However, to start the golf swing with the hands or the hips (i.e. the flail or body unit) is certainly not wrong, but to do this often becomes an invitation to miss out somewhere else on the complete muscular sequence.

A simple analogy of the downswing muscular chain reaction is to regard the three muscular components of the body, shoulders and flail as being equivalent to a 3 stage rocket capable of putting a satellite into orbit (Fig 26). In such a triple combination rocket the initial thrust would be from the enormously powerful main engines which would start the movement from zero and build it up to a critical speed. These engines having completed their task would then fall away and a second group of less powerful engines would take over and boost the rocket speed even further. Eventually, these engines would also fall away and a third and final group of engines would boost the satellite towards its terminal speed, allowing it to escape from the Earth's gravitational field and move into a stable orbit. If any one of the three stages failed or was set off in the wrong sequence, then the final velocity would be insufficient for the satellite to achieve orbit.

The three muscular components of our body, shoulder and wrist musculature are similar to the rocket analogy, and our powerful leg, thigh and body musculature has to initiate the downswing movement which then works up the body and triggers off the shoulder ring into action the final acceleration and control of the clubhead into the ball is achieved by the muscles acting across the wrists.

Anything other than this muscular sequence is failure and the club golfer's common fault of "swinging from the top" means that he has started the downswing sequence with his shoulder or wrist muscles rather than his body musculature. The result of this is disastrous and once such a movement is initiated it immediately cuts off any assistance the powerful body and leg musculature may give to the swing thereafter. To start from the top actually unwinds any tension that might have been generated initially in the body and leg musculature and to undertake a swing such as this is rather like starting the three stage rocket from the ground with the second or final phase engines and leaving the powerful main engines behind. Orbital velocity could never be achieved by such a sequence and yet it is surprising how many club golfers persist in swinging in this fashion and never change.

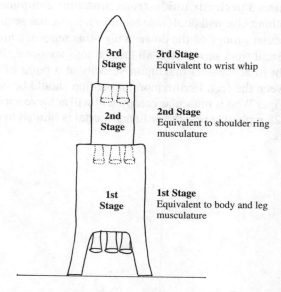

The three rockets may be fueled and assembled in any sequence, but if maximum propulsion and accuracy is to be achieved then they must be fired in the set sequence of Stage 1, Stage 2 and Stage 3 - No other sequence will suffice.

Figure 26 Sequence of muscular contraction on the downswing

Important though the sequence of muscular action is, it is also vital to remember that it is equally important in the centralised Y or *"Theoretically Ideal"* set-up that each of the three muscular groups functions within itself as a unidextrous, balanced and integrated unit. Many right side dominant individuals may actually set up their skeletal components correctly in the first instance; they may even be aware of the correct muscular sequences required; but if their musculature remains right side dominant, then their subsequent mechanical movements will depart more and more from that of the classic swing. That, unfortunately, is how 68% of us go about our task of swinging a golf club.

Therefore the message from these two chapters on skeletal and muscular mechanics is that what I have called the *"Theoretically Ideal"* Y set-up or centralised swing is a muscular movement that requires a **perfectly unidextrous muscular component** to motivate it – nothing else will do. It also requires a particular sequence of the three muscular groups on the downswing –this sequence must start from the base and work upwards. If all these things are done, then the club head ought to achieve its maximum velocity at a point of impact mid-way between the feet. Furthermore, repetition should be easy.

Tiger Woods muscular component will achieve a maximum velocity of 128 mph, whereas the ordinary mortal is limited to the 80 to 90 mph range.

Chapter 5A

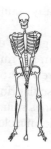

Summary of Chapter 5 – Muscular Mechanics
(Droopy shoulders are the key)

The essential point about the muscular mechanics is that if they are to motivate the skeletal framework to undertake the *"Theoretically Ideal"* or *Y set-up* swing, then it requires that they must work in a unidextrous fashion. In other words, they must work in perfect harmony, one muscle contracting while the equal and opposite muscle relaxes and is stretched – nothing short of this will suffice.

In simplest terms, the muscular component may be considered as consisting of three elements, a muscular ring, a muscular tube and an active muscular hinge. It is rather like having three muscular motors arranged in sequence with the important point being that individually, they must work in a combined and balanced left and right action, and sequentially (on the downswing) the three muscular units must function in a predetermined order.

Figure 19 (Colour Insert) shows the central muscular motor of the three, the muscular ring. It is a continuous ring of muscles around the shoulders and as such is the common link between the two skeletal units, each skeletal unit also has its own individual muscular motor. One of these muscular motors is what I have called the muscular tube and it is made up of all the muscles that clothe the body and leg skeleton (Fig 20 Colour Insert). The muscular ring is actually the upper part of this muscular tube and as such, is the connecting muscular element of the upper body through to the arm muscles and so down to the hinge of the wrists. It is these latter muscles of the arms and wrists that constitute the third muscular motor.

There is therefore a continuous chain or sequence of muscles that can act from the feet up through the legs, trunk and chest, around the shoulder ring and from there down through the arms and finally acting across the wrists.

The backswing actions that are required of these three groups of muscles are firstly, that the body and leg tube be turned from the ring at the top, leaving the feet in a stable position – i.e. corkscrew action from the top to the bottom of the tube. Secondly, that the muscular ring at the same time must bring the shoulders and shoulder blades round (not merely flexing at the shoulder joints). And thirdly, the muscles must act across the wrists and create the wrist flail angle.

In order to appreciate the workings of these three muscular motors it is perhaps easiest to consider the golf swing as an unfolded version with the arms swung on a horizontal plane as if the ball were perched on a tee at shoulder height (Figure 27A, B & C). In this position it is much easier to appreciate the required muscular actions and their

Figure 27A Unfolded swing set-up

sequence. The muscular tube (i.e. the body and legs) is now rather more vertical than the sitting on the bar stool position; however, the legs must remain flexed and springy. On the backswing the muscular action is to turn from the top of the tube relative to the base. The

*Figure 27B Shoulder ring turning - spiral twist of body muscles
from the top and start of two rod flail angle developing*

*Figure 27C Body power muscles poised and balanced - shoulder
ring turned and two rod flail angle developed*

shoulder ring will do this for us, and of course, at the same time, it will also turn the shoulders and with them, the first rod of the flail. Now provided the club face turns to face vertically upwards as it rotates back in a horizontal plane (very important this as otherwise the left side is excluded from the action), the third group of muscles (i.e. those acting across the wrists) will have no difficulty in creating the required angle between the club and the arms. The muscular action of the golf swing is precisely the same as this unfolded swing (i.e. three points of action – the ring, the tube and the wrists), the only difference is that it has to be set into the correct skeletal framework or set-up position.

Essentially, that is it, that is all that is required of the muscular component on the backswing. A chain of three muscular groups that can work in any sequence that one wishes on the backswing – i.e. wrist first, shoulders first or even the body first. However, while any sequence is permissible on the backswing, it has to be stated that no latitude is allowed in the sequence that is undertaken on the downswing. On the downswing, the muscles of the tube must work from the bottom up. Provided they are able to do this and provided their action is perfectly balanced on the left and right (i.e. cross body, unidextrous action), then the *"Theoretically Ideal"* swing must materialise – that is if the correct Y set-up, or mechanical arrangement of the bones, was achieved at the outset. The power of the final wrist action will depend on the amount of cocking and body and shoulder turning that has been achieved on the backswing.

In the previous chapter I described the requirement of the body, shoulder and wrist downswing muscular sequence as being similar to a three stage rocket boosting a satellite into orbit (Fig 26). One can appreciate that if the middle rocket goes off first in the sequence, it will nullify the effect of the main power rocket stage. In other words, to start one's downswing swing from the shoulders will tend to cut out the power from the thighs and legs. Similarly, to start the downswing with the wrists (i.e. the final stage rocket) will reduce any power impact from either the shoulders or the body. It is therefore important that the downswing sequence is correct if one is to make the most of each muscular group.

While I believe that the vast proportion of club golfers' swing faults develop because their right side musculature becomes dominant over their left, nevertheless there are those who have all the muscular potential at their disposal but destroy it because they get this simple one, two, three downswing sequence in the wrong order.

The other principal muscular fault in my view is to set up with muscles that are too tense – particularly round the shoulders. I like the phrase "droopy shoulders at set-up". To me this is the ideal situation as it allows a full and easy turn of the shoulders and because of that, encourages a unidextrous and relaxed movement throughout the whole swing sequence.

[At this stage I would suggest the reader moves on to the next chapter and only goes back to Chapter 5 if one wishes for more detail on the muscular component, or one feels the summary in this chapter has been rather too brief].

Chapter 6

Functional Variations around the Ideal Theme

So far I have been describing only what I have termed the *"Theoretically Ideal"* swing, the swing which has made use of the Y set-up along with a perfectly unidextrous muscular component. However, it is obvious to all who enjoy watching golf that few of the better players actually use this swing technique. The Reverse K technique is the popular address position and is what could be called the "conventional" set-up. But even here there is a degree of variation amongst the better golfers. The reason why I have spent so much time in describing the *"Theoretically Ideal"* swing is because I regard it as being the objective and fixed reference point that is central to all swings, be they functional or non-functional swings. It is therefore something that we can use to our advantage. If we understand it, then we can use it to analyse, compare and contrast all the other swings from it. It is the centralised ideal concept that we can all refer to and know that each and every one of us is referring to the same thing. It has to be the starting point for the discussion of all swings, as all swings are variants from this basic and centrally balanced concept.

For the remainder of this chapter I will discuss functional swings that vary from this centralised concept. Because of the fact that, in this chapter, I am discussing only functional and effective swings, they will therefore tend to be relatively minor departures from the *"Theoretically Ideal"* concept. For the easier description of these swings it is best to divide them into two types. There are those that are variations "within" the ideal swing, and there are those that are variations "away" from the centralised unidextrous theme. Any one swing may contain either or both variations.

Functional Swing Variations "Within" the Ideal Concept

In the description of the ideal or perfectly unidextrous swing I mentioned that the actual sequence in which the three muscular groups carried out their actions on the backswing was of little importance although I did suggest that to use the muscular ring as the initiator was perhaps the easiest and most logical approach.

Most professional golfers tend to carry out all three movements of cocking their wrists, turning their shoulders and rotating their body and legs at one and the same time, but by no means all do this. Japan's Isao Aoki, America's Fred Couples and Ronan Rafferty are all golfers who make wrist cocking, or controlled folding of the flail angle, as their initial movement, and Nick Faldo tended to practise this movement a lot before he started into his swing in a fairly conventional fashion. Now, although all these players may start their swings by cocking their wrists, they then all go on to complete their full shoulder and body turn and end up at the top of their swings in very much the same muscular and skeletal positions as their more conventional colleagues. However, it does make for a swing that has a distinctive character.

In pre-war days it was accepted that the professional swing was initiated by the body musculature, and a look at many pre-1940 golf books illustrates this point. They describe the initial movement as being that of the right hip moving back and round, and Bobby Jones, Walter Hagen and most of the top players of this era started their swings by a backward movement of the right hip ... in other words, the body muscular component as their swing initiator. Again, a swing that will have a different appearance from that of Aoki & Co., but with much the same position at the top.

The point to appreciate from all this is that whichever of the three muscular groups starts the swing, and even if it is all three muscular groups acting together, it matters very little in the Y set-up provided the concepts of a balanced, unidextrous muscular action takes place and all three groups are correctly primed. The end result at the top of the swing will be precisely the same and the only difference will be that each swing will have a different character. It is really the age old argument of the chicken and the egg and if we look at the rocket analogy (Chapter 5), it is like arguing that it is better to fuel the main rocket first whereas others might argue that one or other of the booster rockets ought to be fuelled first. Pointless discussion: what is clear is that all three rockets must be fuelled and which one is fuelled first in the sequence is of no real consequence. The current method is to emphasise the shoulder ring turn as the primary move and this would seem to make good sense as it is common to both of the other muscular groups. Nevertheless, we must accept that fashions do change and it is possible that this method will be outdated in a few years time, and in this respect we already hear that many top professionals are advocating that we should start the wrist cocking very much earlier in the swing sequence. Such a statement would have been heresy only ten years ago when the one piece takeaway was in fashion. I have no doubt that some bright golfer in the not too far distant future will re-discover that it is absolutely essential to start the swing by undertaking the body movement first!

Figure 28 shows swings with each of the three muscular movements being the initiator, but the end result at the top of the swing is much the same in each case – the same muscles are lengthened and made ready for action. The difference will be that each swing will have its own character.

Figure 28A Hip movement as swing initator

Figure 28B Shoulder turn as swing initiator

Figure 28C Wrist cock as swing initiator

Figure 28D All capable of the same top of the swing position

While it is possible to discuss and have differences of opinion regarding the sequence of backswing movements, there can be no discussion about the sequence of downswing movements. It has to be accepted that the lower body or leg musculature initiates the downswing movement and this muscular movement works its way up the trunk and pulls round the shoulders. As they come round, so the flail action is initiated and this finally whips the club-head into the ball. No variation from this sequence is possible as it is essentially a chain reaction from the legs to the wrists. Having stated this, one would assume that this was all that was necessary to be said on the subject. But oh dear no! Opinions remain divided as to the relative emphasis that a player might put into each of the muscular components. In earlier days, Henry Cotton and his school of thought held that it was the hands and forearms that were the main power elements of the swing. The counter view came from the American school led by such as Tom Weiskopf: he felt it was the muscles of the thighs, legs and lower back that were the main power elements of the downswing.

Who was right and who was wrong?

The answer is much as one would expect. It is that both are right and neither is wrong. What they are really discussing is how they consider the muscular power ought to be distributed between the three rockets, and this is clearly a matter of individual preference. Neither view will conflict in any way with the principle of the ideal swing, nor with the concepts of unidextrous muscular action. It will, however, produce a swing of a distinctive style and appearance. The golfer who places his power source predominantly in one of the three muscular groups will be labelled as a power golfer, whereas the man who allows all three units to work in equal harmony will be described as a classic swinger of the club. Henry Cotton and Billy Casper were two golfers who were very much characterised by their wrist whip into the ball whereas Payne Stewart and Tony Jacklin in his glory days tended to accentuate their lower body to generate power. If I were forced to choose between the two methods I would tend to opt for the Cotton style as I feel that wrist movement is not as damaging an accentuation as lower body emphasis. There is no doubt that backs are vulnerable parts of one's anatomy as one ages. In actual fact, I would advise all but the very best of amateur golfers to shy well away from any muscular accentuation as I am convinced it only leads (for the majority of us) to right side muscular dominance, and that, as we will learn, is the kiss of death to most golf swings. I would therefore say, forget the power stuff, leave that to the professionals and top amateurs. Aim to be like the Sam Snead's, the Peter Thomson's and the Gene Littler's of former days. They were all men who could have used a power start or a sprint finish to their swings if they had wished, but they chose not to as they preferred to allow their swings to develop in an even and balanced fashion, with the result that they all possessed beautiful flowing movements. Young Tiger Woods is the perfect example of tremendous power but beautifully balanced – all three muscular units work in perfect harmony, but also with the extreme of power that is gifted to very few in this world. In other words, his unidextrous level is well-nigh perfect and he can afford to push it to extremes that few other fellow professions can attain without tipping into some left or right side imbalance.

Functional Swing Variations "Away" from the Ideal Theme

This second group of deviant, but none the less functional swings, are swings that could be described as being "away" from, rather than "within" or around the central, unidextrous or ideal concept. This type of swing deviation tends to be indulged in by the majority of tournament players and most of the better golfers – very few top class players in fact play with a Y set-up

In order to understand why this is so, it is necessary to understand the effects that even the slightest degree of right side muscular bias has on the *"Theoretically Ideal"* swing. The initial effect of right side dominance is seen in the action of the Trapezius/Pectoral or shoulder ring of muscles. The result of even a minor degree of right side bias will be to break the mechanical integrity of the base of the 1st rod of the flail unit. In the analogy with the coat-hanger, it is as if the right side of the coat-hanger is folded back while the left side is left to lag behind (Fig 29 Colour Insert). Once this important mechanical constant of the width of the base of the flail unit is smashed, the swing to all intents and purposes is set on a destructive path. It automatically follows that the right side dominant muscular action will continue and flow over into the body and leg muscular tube and the hand and arm musculature, with the result that these two skeletal units will be prevented from carrying out their balanced mechanical action.

In the body and leg skeletal unit, the mechanical consequence of right side dominance is that on the backswing the left knee will break in sharply as control is passed over to the right side musculature and the right side muscles alone will be lengthened and passively stretched (Fig 30A). The result is that none of the powerful body, shoulder and thigh muscles on the left side will be lengthened, stretched and prepared for downswing activity. The muscular tube will tend to act on one side only.

In the flail unit, as we have seen, right side muscular action breaks the integrity of the base, and because of this it will also cause the other two constants of the 1st rod of the flail to also break asunder. The left elbow joint will flex (it has no other choice), the grip will break apart and destroy its hinge mechanism (piccolo grip). The whole unified nature of the 1st rod of the flail will now be destroyed and the system cannot and will not work as a single entity. Control has irretrievably passed over to the right arm and hand, and it alone will now become the functioning 1st rod of the flail.

With control of the 1st rod of the flail invested entirely on the right

Figure 30A Too much weight on the right - will be forced to "hit from the top" and end up falling back at impact as 30B - bent left elbow

Figure 30B Falling back at impact - all due to dominant right side musculature in control. Flail point in front of the left foot where right arm and club are in alignment

side, the result is that a three rod flail system (the third joint being the elbow) has been developed (Fig 30A).The mechanical consequence of this is that it will now NOT unwind into a straight line where the ball is placed – i.e. between the feet. By investing power in the right side of the flail, it has in effect pushed the flail point (i.e. where the right side dominated flail unwinds into a straight line) forward to a point that is near to or in front of the left foot (Fig 31). The mechanical effect on the body as a whole is to produce a situation whereby the body tends to fall back and overbalance at or soon after the point of impact with the ball (Fig 30B).

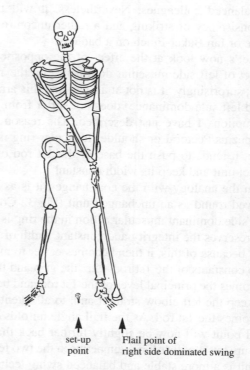

set-up   Flail point of
point   right side dominated swing

***Figure 31 Flail point in a right side dominated swing -
either Y or reverse K set-up***

In this posed picture the actual release point is much further forward than the ball ... it is in line with the right arm. However, we all are forced to hit the ball where it is and that is before the flail has fully unwound. No wonder it is difficult to be either accurate, repetitive or powerful if we use a right side dominant musculature in a framework that was meant to be worked by a unidextrous muscular component!

The amount of right side dominance that the average club golfer develops invariably means complete and utter collapse of the whole swing. However, for the more marginal right side dominant golfer – i.e. those still defined as within the unidextrous range but on the right side of it – their degree of dominance is likely to cause problems, but it will be rather less severe than those of their extremely muscularly unbalanced colleagues. Nevertheless, it will be sufficient to cause inconsistency of striking and a rather uncontrolled game – a bit like Seve or Ian Baker-Finch on a bad day.

Let's now look at the effect of the opposite dominance – i.e. the effect of left side muscular dominance on the Y set-up. Here we find that, surprisingly, it is not at all bad and this arrangement (if it is only mild left side dominance) does not suffer from any of the mechanical disruptions I have just described. The reason for this is that if the Trapezius/Pectoral or shoulder muscular ring is worked from the left side, it tends to push the base of the 1st rod of the flail round as an intact unit and keep its width constant.

In the analogy with the coat-hanger, it is as if the whole hanger is moved round as an unchanged unit (Fig 32 Colour Insert). Moderate left side dominant muscular action in the ring is therefore beneficial as it preserves the integrity and constant width of the base of the 1st rod and because of this, it then becomes easier to maintain intact the other two constants of the 1st rod – i.e. the grip and the height. The left arm becomes the principal lever of the 1st rod, and because of this, it is easy to keep the left elbow straight and, to all intents and purposes, it now becomes the 1st rod. As the flail angle unfolds on the downswing, the flail point will now be slightly further back than in the centralised Y set-up, but it will still remain between the two feet (Fig 33) and the end result is a more stable and balanced swing technique.

Mildly dominant left side muscular action also produces a much better body and leg action as it encourages the joints and larger muscles on the left side to flex rather than hinge, and so help to keep intact the chain or link of passively stretched primed muscles that extend from the wrists to the feet. It therefore encourages the correct development and function of the chain of muscles that will contract to initiate the downswing movement.

To summarise this little diversion into the damaging (or otherwise)

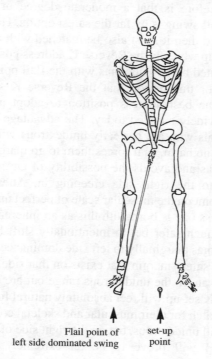

Flail point of set-up
left side dominated swing point

Figure 33
Flail point in a left side dominated swing if Y set-up initially

effects of left or right side muscular dominance on the *"Theoretically Ideal"* swing with its central Y set-up, we can say that only a unidextrous muscular action will completely match with this address position. Any right side muscular bias, however small, will mechanically destroy this set-up. On the other hand, left side bias, up to a certain point, will be acceptable, but even it tends to place the flail point too far back in the stance and there will be a tendency to push the ball at impact. Left side muscular bias will never be quite as destructive as a moderate degree of right side muscular bias, and indeed, left side muscular bias matches well with the Reverse K set-up, as the left arm has already been put in position as the height maintainer of the 1st rod of the flail.

The conclusion therefore is that a moderate degree of left side muscular bias in the golf swing is by far the safest option. However, if it is going to be adopted then it must also be matched with a left side orientated skeletal set-up which is the Reverse K address position. The Y set-up will be disrupted by left side bias with the flail point pushed back. I believe it is for this reason that the Reverse K set-up has become regarded as the best address position to adopt and is the position that is most widely adopted today. The advantage of such a set-up is that individuals who are perfectly unidextrous will find the Reverse K set-up does no harm, as it forces them to go marginally left with their muscular bias and avoids the possibility of any dangerous muscular excursions to the right side creeping in. Attempting to reproduce the single point on the muscular scale of perfect unidexterity is a difficult task (unless one is born with this as an inherent instinct) and it is therefore a much safer bet to intentionally shift both one's muscular and skeletal bias marginally to left side dominance and make use of the much wider safety margin that exists on that side.

For the golfers who are in the unidextrous range but are on the left side of it, the Reverse K set-up will feel absolutely natural for them, as it will be the perfect match for their muscular and skeletal components.

For those that are still unidextrous, but on the right side of the range, the Reverse K set-up will prove to be an extremely beneficial arrangement for them, as the very act of setting up that way gives them a positive and constant reminder each and every time to make sure that they place their left side musculature in control. This must not be a rigid, tense, or excessively dominant left side control, but sufficient to block out any damaging right side muscular excesses. By being in the broad unidextrous range, these players can relatively easily learn to shift their muscular emphasis over to the left, but it will never be quite as easy for them as for the perfect, or marginally left side, unidextrans.

While the Reverse K address position has become accepted as the most functional set-up, it is not the only functional set-up that is possible. There are other skeletal modifications that may be applied to this basic left sided concept. My guess is that most of these

Colour Insert

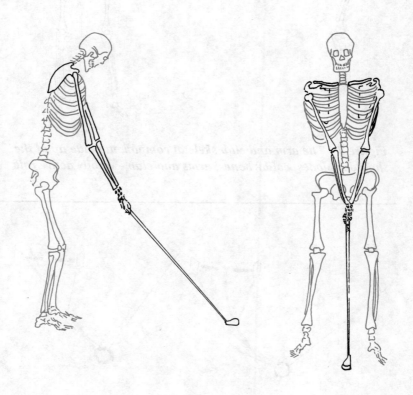

Figure 5 - The head, chest, spine and legs skeletal component (red)
- supportive plus rotational role

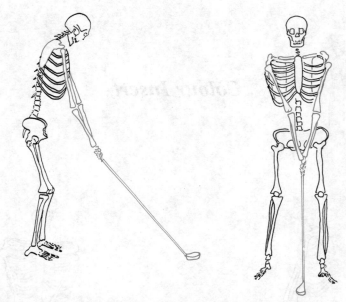

Figure 7 - The arm and club skeletal component made up of the
shoulder blades, collar bones, arms and club - wholly active role

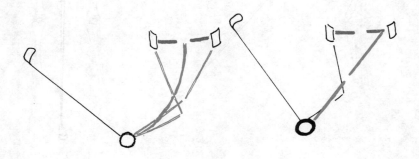

Figure 11 - The three constants of the 1st rod of the flail - the base
(green), the height (red) and the grip (black)

Figure 14 A & B - The maintenance of the three constants of the 1st rod using the Y (A) or reverse K (B) set-up

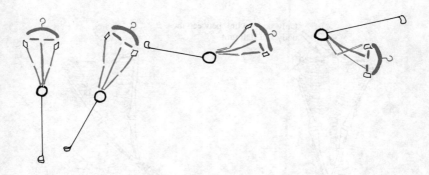

A - The Y set-up - the three constants maintain the 1st rod as an isosceles triangle

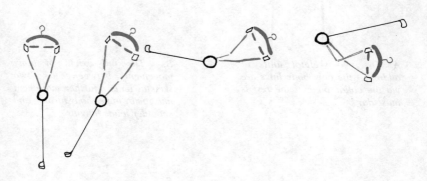

B - The reverse K set-up - the three constants maintain the 1st rod as a right angled triangle

Figure 15 - The mechanical link between the two skeletal units

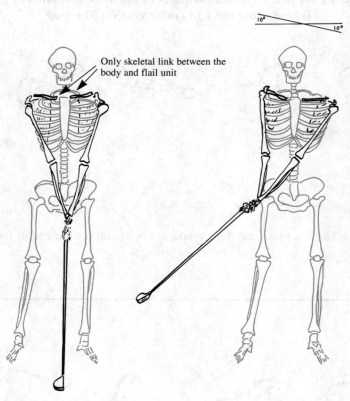

Only skeletal link between the body and flail unit

A. *The two skeletal units at address - the only bony links are via the collar bones - the rest is muscular*

B. *The full extent of bony movement between the two skeletal units - further movement must be by upper body turning and shoulder joints hinging*

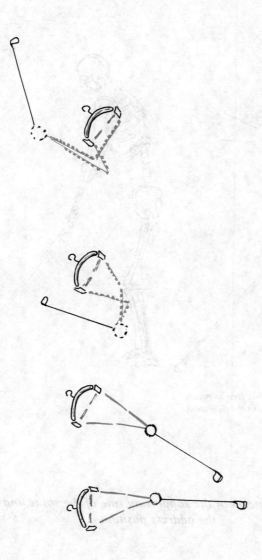

Figure 16 - Hinging of the shoulder joints - no effective link with the body skeletal complex - shoulders (i.e. coat-hanger) have not turned (cf. Figure 14B)

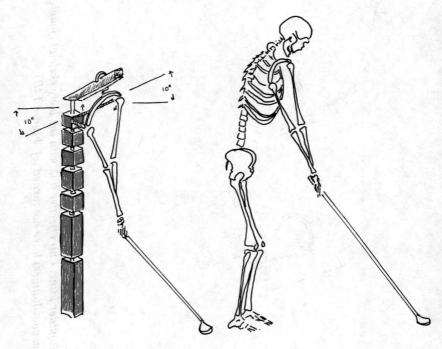

Base of active unit only free to rotate
some 10 degrees unless the flail post
(spine) also turns.

**Figure 17 - Concept of the supporting role of the spine and legs -
the address position**

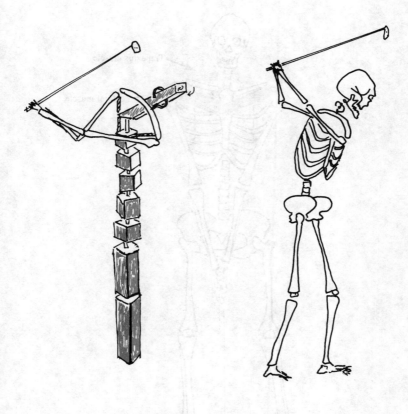

Upper spine and chest turned from fixed base - two rod flail primed.

Figure 18 - Concept of the spine and legs, supportive plus active role

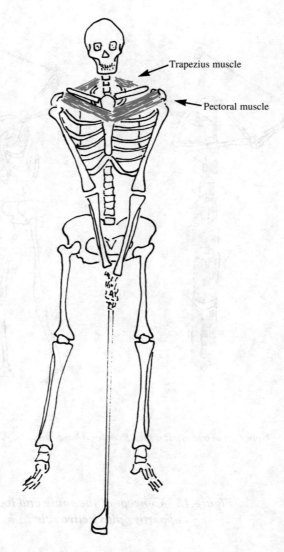

Trapezius muscle

Pectoral muscle

Figure 19 - The shoulder (Trapezius/Pectoral) muscular swing - the vital link between the two skeletal units

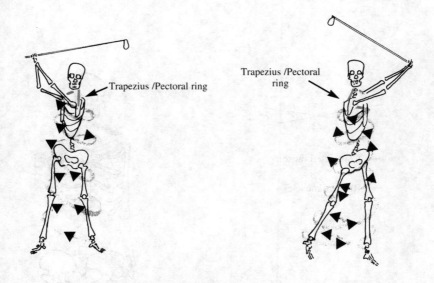

**Figure 20 - The body and leg muscular component "descending"
from the Trapezius/Pectoral ring – backswing and downswing**

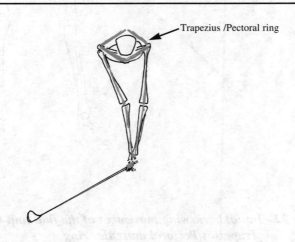

**Figure 21 - The flail muscular component "ascending" from the
Trapezius/Pectoral ring (view from above)**

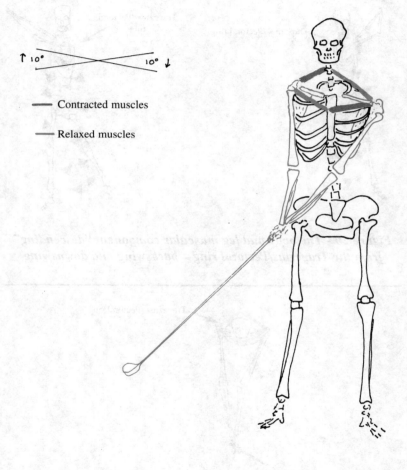

Figure 22 - Initial backswing movement of the flail unit by Trapezius/Pectoral muscular ring

Lumbar and thoracic
spine almost straight
allowing ease of
rotation and
maintenance of support
for the neck spine -
shoulders over the base
of the feet

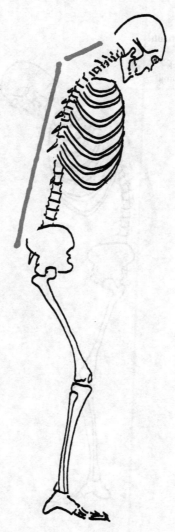

Figure 23 - Correct Spinal Posture

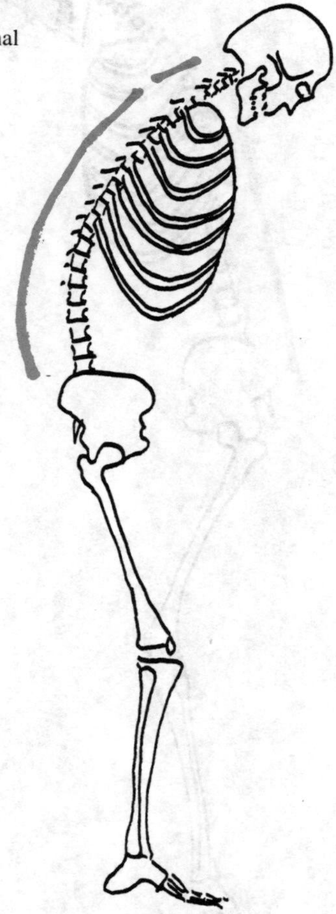

Rounded back, difficult
to maintain good
support for the neck
spine - cramped spinal
turning

Figure 24 - Poor Spinal Posture

Spine tilted too far
forward beyond the
base of the feet.
Necessitates use of back
and thigh muscles that
would be more
beneficially used in
carrying out their
primary roles

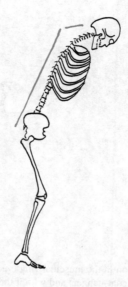

Figure 25A - Poor Leg Posture

Too erect, does not
allow the flail unit to
suspend properly -
restricts body turning

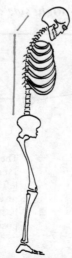

Figure 25B - Poor Leg Posture

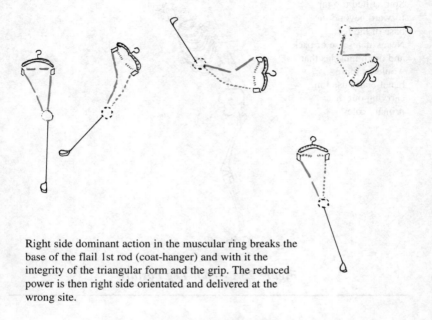

Right side dominant action in the muscular ring breaks the
base of the flail 1st rod (coat-hanger) and with it the
integrity of the triangular form and the grip. The reduced
power is then right side orientated and delivered at the
wrong site.

Figure 29 - Right side dominant swing

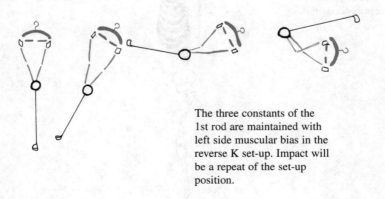

The three constants of the
1st rod are maintained with
left side muscular bias in the
reverse K set-up. Impact will
be a repeat of the set-up
position.

Figure 32 - Effect of left side muscular bias on the flail unit

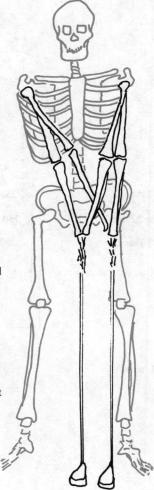

Range of skeletal component from Y to Reverse K set-up. Plus Trevino-like adaptations will produce a functional swing. However, both muscular and skeletal components must be in harmony.

Range of muscular component that best fits with the Y to Reverse K set-up is from perfect unidextrous to all the left side of the unidextrous range, i.e. the four left-hand side columns of Figure 3A-P29.

Figure 35 - The range of muscular and skeletal components that combine to produce "A Perfect Swing"

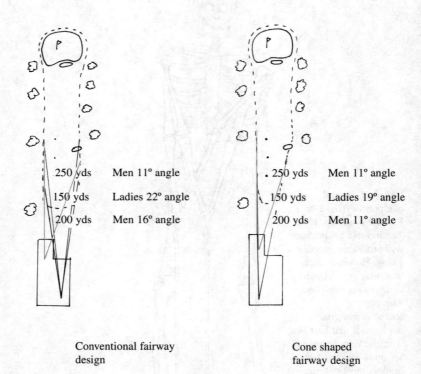

Conventional fairway
design

Cone shaped
fairway design

Figure 41 - Cone shaped fairway design

modifications are indulged in by golfers who are at the more extreme range of the right side of the unidextrous zone, and the most obvious example of this amongst the past or present professionals must surely be Lee Trevino with his open stance and unique swing movement which makes the wrists go under and through at impact with the intention of keeping the club face square to the ball for a much longer period (Fig 34).

There are also many other excellent golfers who possess their own individual variations of the "Reverse K" set-up. Bernhard Langer, John Daly and David Duval use extremely strong left hand grips while Gary Player was one who made his left elbow ramrod stiff. These golfers, and many like them, have instinctively found the skeletal alteration to the Reverse K address position that is correct for them and that has allowed them to harmonise their slightly out of balance musculature with the particular and unique set-up and swing movement that they find gives them power and consistency. Such an altered skeletal set-up may force them to become habitual "faders" or "drawers" of the ball and players who will tend to shy away from the opposing shot. But the point is that the adoption of a slightly different set-up or swing movement from the centralised concept has not denied any of them a

Figure 34A Trevino style set-up Reverse K and slightly open stance

Figure 34B
Trevino style impact position - Left side of flail in firm control

balanced, powerful and repetitive flail stroke. Each professional golfer with a slightly off-beat swing has found harmony between his muscular and skeletal component. I have little doubt that to have forced many of these players to have conformed to an absolutely classic Reverse K set-up and grip (or even worse, a Y set-up) would undoubtedly have made life much more difficult for them.

It is therefore possible to have an almost infinite variety of swing modifications (Fig 35 Colour Insert) that are extremely functional and exist in the range between the partial left side muscular dominance set-up (i.e.Reverse K set-up) and the perfect unidexterity set-up (i.e. the Y set-up). If one also adds to these muscular variations those that are "within" the ideal swing then it can readily be seen why there is such a variety of swings on view at any professional tournament.

The corollary to all this would seem to be that it must surely be a flawed concept to attempt to train all aspiring golfers along one pathway, and in this respect it does seem that more individualistic swings are seen on the tournament circuit than has been the case for a number of years.

Chapter 7

Less Acceptable Variations around the Theme – Handicap Swings

By use of the phrase "handicap swings", I refer to swings that are reduced in effectiveness but are not necessarily bad or faulty swings in the sense that every stroke is a destructive shot. On the contrary, many handicap swings can be extremely skilfully performed and may be capable of repetitive and consistent play. Indeed, if they can be allied to a sound short game it may be possible for a golfer to play to an upper single figure handicap. They will, however, be swings that are limited in terms of length or ball control and are unlikely to produce a low single figure or scratch golfer.

In the last chapter I explained why I believed that right side muscular dominance was the most frequent cause of swing failure (or left side dominance in the left hander). But it is certainly not the only reason and there must be many golfers who are in possession of excellent muscular potential (i.e. they have unidextrous ability) but either through lack of application, poor hand/eye co-ordination, or because they are afflicted with a degree of restricted joint movement, fail to get past the starting gate with their swings and fail to capitalise on their inherent muscular potential.

In order to look at some of the problems associated with handicap swings it is convenient to divide them into three categories and their sub-groups. Quite obviously, one fault will lead to another and only rarely will any particular handicap swing drop precisely into one or other of the three categories. However, a description along these lines gives a useful insight into some of the principles that are involved, and will help in the next chapter when we look at how some of these problem swings that afflict club golfers may be rectified. The three categories with their sub-groups are:–

Category 1

Mechanical Faults

Faults that are due to a lack of understanding, or misconception, of how the golf swing ought to function. There is no inherited muscular or skeletal fault.

   (i) Incomplete sequence of movement golfer
- Use of flail unit only.
- Body & shoulder, no flail.

  (ii) Wrong sequence of movement golfer
- The uncocker.
- The shoulder ring initiator.

Category 2

Skeletal Faults

Reduced swing efficiency because of poor genetic or acquired skeletal material, or incorrect setting of the skeletal framework prior to starting the swing. No inherited muscular fault.

Category 3

Muscular Faults

Faults in the swing that are due to the possession of a side dominant muscular component that remains uncorrected or uncompensated.

   (i)   Right side muscular dominance.

  (ii)   Left side muscular dominance.

Category 1

Mechanical Faults

     Handicap Swings resulting from a lack of understanding of the
       full range of mechanical movements required

    I assume that this group are unidextrous golfers who have the muscular potential to become excellent low handicap players with functional swings but for some reason or another they have not summoned up enough interest to learn the basic sequences of the golf swing. In other words, their muscular component is satisfactory and it will do the job for them, but their downfall lies in the fact that they have failed to learn the basic mechanics of the swing. Their favoured method of play is to either select one or two components of the classic swing and limit their play to the use of these movements, or else make a correct backswing movement but then perform the downswing movement in the wrong sequence.

(i) The Incomplete Sequence of Movement Golfer
  There are two types in this sub-group:-
- *The Flail Unit Golfer* – This golfer tends to limit his swing movements to the flail action alone and has limited shoulder turn and little or no body movement (Fig 36, compare with Fig 28 A &

Figure 36 Golfer with flail action but little shoulder or body action

C). He will form a flail angle between the two rods, but then fails to go on and develop the full backswing movement because of limited shoulder and upper body turn.

As far as this golfer's muscular component is concerned and the analogy of the rocket, it is as if he is using almost no main rocket and a severely restricted first stage booster. He tries to work his swing almost entirely from his final booster rocket – i.e. his wrists and shoulder joints with a little help from a shoulder turn which would bring in the powerful body muscles.

It must be said that this swing, if well performed, is unidextrous in action and it can be repetitive. However, it is only using a portion of the muscle power available and as a result will lack length. Nevertheless, these golfers do keep plugging the ball up the middle of the fairway and as there is very little to go wrong with it, most of them will perform in the 12 to 18 handicap range. Only rarely do they get down to single figure handicaps.

- *The Body and Shoulder Golfer, no Flail* – This reduced swing movement is also one that a potentially unidextrous golfer might fall into. The fault is to perform the body and shoulder turn satisfactorily but miss out on the wrist cock and flail angle. As likely as not this golfer (Fig 37) will have read somewhere that he must keep his left arm straight and he misinterprets this to mean that he has to keep the left arm plus the club in a straight line throughout the whole swing.

Figure 37 Golfer with minimal flail action

In the rocket analogy it is as if this golfer has used the main and first stage rockets but has completely ignored the final booster. His (or more frequently her) swing comes out as a rather slappy, sweeping motion. He (or she) is often a reasonably consistent player with woods (but will never be noted for length) and is a golfer who is unable to punch iron shots into greens. Woods will be preferred to medium or long irons.

Both these swing types are capable of being unidextrous swings but they are deficient in one or more of the muscular sequences of the classic swing and because of this are reduced in effectiveness and low handicap golf will never be played on average length courses. On the other hand, they have the merit of being fairly consistent handicap swings.

(ii) Wrong Sequence of Movement Golfer

* This golfer, like the two we have just seen, may also have unidextrous muscular potential, but their fault is that they get their sequence of muscular movements in the wrong order on the downswing. They get to the top of the backswing reasonably well by priming the three muscular groups but then choose the wrong muscular sequence to trigger off the downswing. Two wrong sequences are possible.

* *The Uncocker* – This golfer gets to the top of the backswing correctly, but then commits the cardinal sin of starting the

Figure 38A Reasonable top of swing position

***Figure 38B Downswing has started by "throwing from the top"
i.e. unwinding the flail first***

downswing with the uncocking of the wrists as the initial movement
(Fig 38). The effect of this is disastrous as it promptly destroys the
whole aim and purpose of the backswing which has been to prime
the three muscular groups. By use of the flail unit as the initiator of
the downswing, this golfer is placing himself in a very similar
position to the golfer who has failed to form the flail angle in the
first place. In actual fact, he is rather worse off, as he now has to
contend with the added burden of the other two primed muscular
groups still trying to produce power and get in on the downswing
act. In doing so, they achieve little more than additional skeletal
imbalance and end up spinning out into the classic "Reverse C"
impact position.

It is as if this golfer has used the final rocket booster as the initiator
of the whole movement and is then desperately trying to catch up the
released pay-load with the other two rockets.

• *The Shoulder, Ring Initiator* – The only other faulty muscular
  sequence possible, if the correct backswing has been achieved
  initially, is to start the downswing with the shoulder ring as the

Figure 39A Shoulders have turned but body muscles have not been used - still some flail to come

Figure 39B Impact, but body and legs have played little part

initiator (Fig 39). This, as with the "uncocker", is also disruptive and is equivalent to setting the first stage rocket off initially and hoping the main engine will catch up later. It is marginally more balanced than the "uncocker's" swing but neither of these golfers will be as consistent and balanced in play as the two golfers in the first group who only primed and then used a limited part of their swing sequence.

In all these four examples it has been possible for the golfers to have a unidextrous muscular capability and their only mistake is that they have erred in a mechanical sense by missing out on a particular sequence, or of getting the sequences in the wrong order. It is, of course, also possible to compound these errors with skeletal set-up faults and/or left or right side muscular bias.

Category 2

Skeletal Faults

Handicap Swings resultant on incorrect setting of the skeletal framework prior to starting the swing.

If the "theoretically ideal" swing is to be undertaken, then it requires that the system of joints and levers is set up in the correct position prior to starting the swing – i.e. the Y set-up. Failure to do this would be rather like setting the ailerons or rudder of a twin engined plane at various acute angles and hoping that a balanced action from the two engines would still fly the plane straight. In other words, an improbable combination.

Nevertheless, having said this, all competent golfers do use this technique in a controlled fashion in order to manipulate the ball and make it fade, draw or go high or low. In other words, they will open or close their stance to enable them to impart spin to the ball, or change the angulation of the club face at impact to give either more or less loft. In these ways the flight of a ball may be controlled. There are many top class golfers who have introduced a skeletal bias into their game as a permanent feature, and the late Bobby Locke with his closed stance and weird but consistent hooking shot was perhaps the best example of this. This is not, however, handicap golf – this is the higher realms of ball control as practised by the best exponents of the game.

The golfer I refer to in this section is the golfer who has all the muscular potential at his disposal but yet aligns his skeleton in such a manner that he inhibits any possibility of his muscles being able to perform the correct sequence of movements. This has to be a minority group as it must be difficult to imagine any person who is highly muscularly competent not getting the information feedback from either the ball's flight or the proprioception from his own muscles that would not automatically make him alter his maligned grip or set-up and move towards a skeletal arrangement that would afford better power and control. Virtually all good golfers who "go off the boil" do in fact come into this category and good tutors know that all that is needed for these class golfers is a "five minute fix". In other words, their muscular components are acting correctly and it needs no change. However, their skeletal component has gone very slightly out of alignment and once replaced in the correct position it will then allow the power and accuracy to return.

This group also contains the golfers who may have skeletal defects (congenital or acquired) which limit the range of movement of their joints. An example would be a golfer with an arthritic neck condition. Because of this he would be totally unable to provide a good mechanical link between his flail unit and his body unit, not because the muscles will not work, but merely because the spine will not turn.

Apart from the golfers with skeletal defects, all the players in the above two categories should be responsive to conventional tuition, as they possess a muscular component with good potential.

Category 3

Muscular Faults

> *Handicap swings resultant from the possession of a faulty muscular component that is excessively right or left side dominant – this muscular fault will inevitably spill over into a combined muscular and skeletal fault.*

(i) The Right Side Dominant Golfer

- In the last chapter I described how, if a golfer set himself up in the *"Theoretically Ideal"* set-up position (or even the reverse K), and then used a right side dominant musculature (and remember 68% of us have an almost instinctive inclination to do so), THEN THE MAINTENANCE OF SKELETAL UNITY THROUGHOUT THAT SWING MOVEMENT BECOMES IMPOSSIBLE. It is because of this that it is an instinctive and natural reaction for such golfers to abandon the classic set-up position and seek a skeletal set-up and grip that they sense will match rather better their particular muscular dominance.

This problem, in one form or another, afflicts the vast majority of club golfers. Present day accepted teaching methods force their skeletal component into a particular position that is not in harmony with their muscular component, and the plain fact is that "muscles will be satisfied", and that they will take precedence over the skeletal component. If, however, a golfer is possessed of good hand/eye co-ordination and is prepared to accept the somewhat ungainly style of swing that results, then it is possible (if the right side dominance is not too excessive) to produce a swing method that will compete in the middle handicap range and even occasionally get down to single figures (much as I did as a student). It will, however, be a limited technique, it will never look satisfactory, it will never achieve good length and a golfer performing in this fashion will invariably be an inconsistent golfer from tee to green.

(ii) The Left Side Dominant Golfer

- I explained how marginally left side dominant golfers, but still within the unidextrous range, are in the most fortunate situation of all, and they should adopt the Reverse K address position as it is the perfect match for their muscular component. There are, however, some 4 percent of the population who are beyond the unidextrous range and are so left side dominant that they are invariably forced to play their golf left handed. If they do this, they then have precisely the same problems as the dominant right side golfers.

Analysis and understanding by the player concerning the reasons for failure is, in my view, the only way to bring about improvement in the poorer player with either a right or left side dominant bias problem. I suggest it is the prevailing lack of in-depth knowledge as to their reasons for failure that is the biggest hurdle to be overcome by modern golf tuition. The conveniently held belief that if a method works for a professional then it must work for Joe Bloggs is a difficult one to break down, but I would hope that I have been able to show why this has to be faulty reasoning, and why, if something is to be done about it, then a more rational and logical approach to the teaching of these players at the middle and upper end of the handicap scale has to be achieved.

Chapter 8

The Way Forward

If we can now accept that there are mechanical swing faults, muscular swing faults, and faults that are a combination of both, then it would seem illogical that the correction of all these three faults should be approached in precisely the same way. Modern golf tuition has tended to do this by relying on mechanical instruction to be its sole vehicle to modify and correct the whole range of faults ... with the idea being that a constant repetition of the correct mechanical movements will, in the end, train the body's muscles to memorise and repeat these movements ad infinitum.

I am not convinced that this is a valid assumption and I make the suggestion that faults that are of muscular origin should be dealt with at source and not indirectly through skeletal mechanics. I do not say mechanical instruction is of no use, but I do say that an environment should be created whereby this form of tuition can have a better chance of being successful than it does at the moment. Few teaching professionals are likely to disagree with this sentiment and many of them do actually go along this path when they make strenuous efforts to get their pupils to relax during a lesson. I suspect this is rarely done with the full realisation of the precise physiological necessity of getting their pupils to function within, or on the left side of, their muscular unidextrous range. Nevertheless, it is often sufficient to drop them into a muscularly functional zone and render them more receptive to the mechanical instruction that is being given. However, the disadvantage with this approach to tuition is that the minute the lesson is over and the pupil is on his own again, then the lust for power comes to the fore and any instinctive right side muscular dominance automatically reasserst itself. The end result is that short term gain is rarely sustained and translated into long term effectiveness.

The more perspicacious of golf tutors have appreciated these problems and the more imaginative ones amongst them have sought for other and better ways to train their pupils' muscles to perform at a consistent and repetitive level.

I once read of a teacher who made his pupils "run on the spot" for five minutes before he allowed them to hit a ball. This was his method of releasing tension and producing a relaxed and balanced muscular component. It is certainly a novel way of approaching the task of achieving muscular relaxation and body balance. However, I am rather uncertain as to how the majority of members (particularly the ladies) would react if their club professional instructed them to do five minutes jogging on the spot before they were allowed to hit a practice ball. I think most of us would assume the pro had lost his marbles at a relatively young age. That is, if we hadn't already had a coronary by the third or fourth minute into our callisthenics! Maybe all right for the young and fit on the practice ground but not for everyday use.

I also heard of another professional's approach to the problem wherein he instructing his pupils to "listen to the swing" as they hit the ball. His advice was to listen to the swish of the shaft and the strike of the clubhead on the ball at impact. I give full credit to this instructor for thinking up an extremely clever and intelligent way of diverting his pupils' attention from power and swing mechanics and putting it all into the striking of the ball as sweetly and as repetitively as possible. The real advantage of this method is that it is directly aimed at the muscles and is therefore likely to stay with the pupil long after the lesson is over.

Other gimmicks that have been used are mostly concerned with rhythm, and advice to swing to the beat of the Blue Danube Waltz, or to breath in on the backswing and out on the downswing, or even to think of the one word "tempo", are all ploys that have been used to moderate the destructive effects of a right side dominant musculature.

The trouble with all these methods is that they do not provide a permanent solution to the problem and I am convinced that, if you are right side dominant, then without insight into the real reasons for your failure, a permanent cure is unlikely.

My suggestion for a new approach to the teaching (or learning) of the golf swing is therefore based on the belief that there has to be a conscious and rational understanding of the reasons for failure (both by the professional and the pupil). I am convinced that only by being taught (and understanding) the actual reasons for a personal swing failure will it be possible to do anything to correct that fault on a permanent basis. In other words, the conscious brain has to be the medium that initiates a swing change if a muscular re-orientation is required. But before it does this, it must be aware of the instructions that it has to give to the muscles.

In putting forward this suggestion I am not abandoning the present methods of tuition. There is nothing wrong with mechanical tuition, and indeed, it has to be the starting point for everyone and will remain the only correct method for the golfer endowed with unidextrous potential. Every golfer must learn the correct set-up and grip initially and be shown and understand the basic fundamentals of the swing sequence. It is absolutely right to do this and indeed, I would encourage use of all the mechanical training devices that are available to help in this. These might include video playback, clubs with pre-moulded grips, clubs that produce a "click" if swung correctly, clubs that have a joint in the shaft, straps placed across the upper arms, a football between the arms, towels tucked under the armpits, and even hoops that mould the swing plane. These gimmicks all have their place as they all stress some important mechanical aspect of the functional swing. However, it must be realised that while all these devices have every chance of being successful in the unidextrous individual (and I must say I am surprised they are not used more in the average lesson), they will be of much more limited value to the golfers who are trapped in a right side dominant muscular component. Progress for these pupils will be extremely slow or non-existent unless their errant muscular components can be changed to conform to the skeletal technique that is being used. Or, if this method does not work, then a change of the skeletal technique to match with the errant muscular component is an alternative way forward.

Whatever path one adopts, it is important initially to understand the simple mechanics of the golf swing and appreciate the joints that are involved. Essentially, they are the body and legs working as a tube with the shoulder blades and upper chest turning equally. Also an understanding that the flail is a two rod system that works from the shoulder blades (plus joints), the left arm and the wrists. Appreciation that the elbows do not take any active part in the swing apart from establishing and maintaining the length of the first rod is important. This latter point is the downfall for most golfers who take up the game from other sports that do include the right or left elbow as a vital and active part of the mechanics of their sport – e.g. squash, tennis or cricket.

I therefore put the following thoughts forward as to how the poorer player may be taught :-

1) Adopt a conventional left side biased skeletal set-up (the Reverse K set-up), but learn to damp down the whole right side musculature to such an extent that the left side of the body and left arm take predominant control of the backswing.

2) Go along the same muscular path (i.e. a more relaxed right side musculature), but make it somewhat easier for the left side to keep control by adopting additional skeletal modifications at the set-up and a slightly different swing technique that will assist the left side musculature in its control of the flail.

3) Move totally away from all convention and adopt a right side dominant set-up and swing technique and match it with a right side dominant musculature.

1) Reverse K Set-up with Left Side Muscular Bias.

The reasoning behind this approach is that the single point of the "Theoretically Ideal" swing is, I believe, too difficult to achieve and sustain for any right side dominant individual. It is therefore better to go for a left side muscular bias, which is a range rather than a defined point, and match this with an appropriate skeletal framework – i.e. the Reverse K set-up. I believe the instructor must explain to the pupil the reasoning behind all this, and the pupil for his part must understand what is being explained. I am convinced that only by intelligent understanding and insight into the skeletal and muscular problems can there be a positive and sustained improvement. It must be an intellectual decision by the pupil to relax his right side musculature and to switch control over to the left side. One hopes that the continual reinforcement of this intellectual decision will come from improved performance on the course.

The opposite approach of exercising and strengthening the weaker left side to bring it up to that of the dominant right side or beyond, would seem to recommend itself as being a better and perhaps more logical way of going about things. Certainly one sees this advice repeated over and over again by competent golfers and teaching professionals in their magazine articles and books. I agree that this approach is likely to be effective for the natural (but unpractised) unidextran, but it will NOT be effective for the 68% of right side dominant individuals. I believe they have no alternative other than to relax their dominant right sides first of all if they wish to harmonise their musculature with the Reverse K set-up and achieve any effective (and necessary) left side control in the swing.

The method of achieving right side muscular relaxation is to start at the right hand and wrist, go on to the right elbow, the right shoulder, the right hip and the right knee; all these joints must be consciously relaxed until a sense of body unity develops and there becomes an awareness that the body, arms and legs are coming together as one. The weight should fall squarely on the feet, the body should feel reasonably tall, the shoulders mobile, almost droopy. The important thing is then to actually overdo this right side relaxation and actually pass the muscular control over to the left side of the body, and particularly the left arm.

The next step is to fine tune the Reverse K set-up and make sure the grip is correct. This has to be the job of the expert. I would only stress that in my opinion the nearer the left arm is to the vertical at the address position, the easier it is for the right side dominant individual to continually restrain his dominant side from taking overall control of the swing and feel that the left arm is live and active.

The stage should now be reached of a marginally left side dominant skeletal set-up clothed with a muscular component which is in harmony with it. The whole right side ought to feel as if it is somehow tucked in behind the left and will not (what I can best describe as) climb outside it once the swing starts.

The ever present danger in the right side dominant individual will always remain of the golfer adopting the Reverse K set-up and failing to match it with the appropriate musculature. It will always remain a natural instinct for this player to switch his power back over to the dominant side, especially if he hasn't played for some time, or else is straining for power. If this is done it will immediately destroy the swing even though the set-up remains that of a Reverse K. There is a world of difference between a mechanical set-up position that is in harmony with a muscular component and a set-up that may appear to be mechanically similar, but is matched with a muscular component that is not in harmony with it. The former will be a set-up that will not only look correct but it will have every chance of acting correctly. The latter will be a set-up that has been achieved despite an unbalanced muscular component and although it may have the superficial appearance of being correct, it will skeletally destruct as soon as any movement takes place. Both set-ups may therefore appear similar, but they will be poles apart from any functional point of view. This will be the ever present danger for at least 68% of the golfing population.

There simply has to be skeletal and muscular harmony and that is what is so often missing in simple mechanical instruction. It is no good a tutor putting the pupil's fingers in the correct grip: they must, in addition, be given the correct muscular component to clothe that grip so that it will maintain its position during function. I believe the unfolded swing (Fig 27) is the ideal teaching vehicle – it is simple to use and appreciate all the component parts of the full swing.

2) Modified Skeletal Set-up with Left Side Biased Muscular Technique.

There are many handicap players who are so excessively right side dominant that they may find it exceedingly difficult to follow the above path. These golfers may find it helpful to adopt additional skeletal modifications to the Reverse K set-up. I have already mentioned Bernhard Langer's, David Duval's and John Daly's strong left hand grips and further examples of these skeletal modifications are seen in the techniques adopted by Arnold Palmer and to a lesser extent, Seve Ballesteros in his younger days. Lee Trevino, however, must be credited with the most extreme example of the type of skeletal modification I refer to.

If we look at Lee Trevino's set-up (Fig 34A), it is in fact a Reverse K set-up but with the addition of an open stance and a modified wrist flail technique through the ball. I would certainly recommend that all right side dominant golfers read Trevino's book wherein he describes his swing technique. I would say, however, it ought to have the proviso attached to it that all who try it must relax their right sides and permit the left side to be in control of the backswing. I believe his set-up technique makes things very much easier for the right side dominant individual.

There is another book that a club golfer called Mindy Blake wrote in 1972. He entitled his book "The Golf Swing of the Future" and in it he described what he felt was the golf swing we should all move towards. Unfortunately for him it did not come to pass, and I think, for one or two very good reasons. What I feel Mindy Blake actually described in his book was not a swing that could be adopted by the best but a set-up and swing method that was of use to right side dominant golfers provided they relaxed their right side at address and put their left in equal or dominant control. He forgot to mention this point. I believe his work was otherwise sound and it should be accepted for what it is and given its due place in golfing literature. I am sure many teaching professionals could, with benefit, study both his book and Trevino's and adapt their methods to pupils where they think it is appropriate. There is absolutely nothing wrong with such off-beat swings provided that both the pupils and the instructors appreciate why they are following these different styles of swings. If the end result is a functional and repetitive swing then a successful conclusion has been reached.

I have no intention of going into detail concerning Mindy Blake's or Lee Trevino's advice except to say that the open stance and the techniques they advise are useful skeletal ploys which make left side muscular control and right side subjugation much easier to achieve. The open stance necessitates a slightly different wrist action through the ball that keeps the club face square through the impact area for a longer period than is normal with the conventional swing. This extension of the swing path through the ball requires a wrist action that forces the right hand under rather than over, and prevents the right hand, and indeed the whole right side of the body, from climbing and rolling over the left side at impact (Fig 34). It is very much an anti-hooking device and this is why Trevino's natural shot is a fade.

The important point about all these set-up modifications is that they make left side control of the flail and flail point much easier to accomplish. They do allow more right side power into the shot, but it must always be right side power that is controlled and harnessed by the left.

3) An Unconventional Right Side Dominant Swing.

If a golfer finds he cannot or does not wish to switch his muscular control over to the left side, the question is, is there anything left for him to try? To attempt (as nearly every high handicap player does) and persist with a right side dominant musculature set in a left side skeletal framework is not and never will be acceptable. This cannot work. Logic suggests that if a golfer is not prepared to compromise and modify his defective muscular component, then there is one further possibility to attempt that must surely be better than persisting with an unbalanced partnership.

The set-up that would seem to make sense for a right side dominant individual is one that could be called the K position set-up. In this set-up (Fig 40) the right arm and club is made into the straight line release of the flail system and the flail angle unwinds in a direct line from the right shoulder to the ball. The ball is placed opposite the right foot (or just inside) with the stance reasonably square. The golfer should unashamedly work his swing from the right shoulder and use his right side musculature. The trick at the address position is to keep the right shoulder pulled back and high, and to break the right wrist initially, and then the right elbow. This forces the right elbow down, rather than letting it fly out. The backswing occurs from the right shoulder with

Figure 40 The K-set-up which fits with a right side dominant musculature. Ball placed opposite the right foot

the passive muscle elongation and lengthening occurring up and down the right side from the right foot to the right wrist. The left shoulder remains relaxed and swings across the chest.

The downswing should be a chain of muscular action from the right knee and thigh with the thrust working up the body and triggering off the flail action – the aim being to produce a late uncocking of the flail angle with the right arm and the club ending in a straight line, with the point of impact occurring opposite the right foot, or just in front. The right shoulder does not come through at impact, it stays back and high. The left side and arm does virtually nothing; they merely go along for the ride.

I am afraid such a swing will be ridiculed by the professionals, but believe me, it does feel natural to a dominant right sided individual. It does makes sense, and it can be reasonably powerful and repetitive. I once played with it for a year and maintained a 5 handicap. The difficult part about this swing is that the bending right elbow introduces an extra joint into the 1st rod of the flail system and it is difficult at first to keep the right shoulder back at impact. However, the player soon gets the knack of straightening out the elbow at impact and working the action from the pulled back right shoulder. Once they appreciate the mechanics involved, the swing can be a pleasure and a delight to play, mainly because for the first time ever, it feels natural to the right side dominant individual.

I certainly don't recommend this swing, but common sense dictates that it is a possibility if all else fails and a golfer is not prepared, or finds it too difficult, to compromise on his right side muscular dominance. This swing gives hope where there was none before and it certainly feels capable of repetition to the occasional golfer. It makes sense as it matches both the muscular and skeletal components.

One or two of my friends have read this chapter and have expressed some disappointment with it. They have felt I have not been detailed enough about the actual swing techniques. I accept this, but I am not a golf teacher, that is not my role, nor is this a book on golf tuition. It is a book on the principles behind swing techniques and my aim is to provide a reasoned insight into the golf swing, how it is performed by the experts, and why it is not performed well by the fallible and imperfect human beings that most of us are.

My purpose is to show the scope and range of the subject and the fact that it is not a simplistic single entity that faces the club golfer (or the teaching professional). It is indeed a complex series of skeletal and muscular variables that exist for most of us, and the correct match must be sought for each individual. I hope I have shown the various paths that each of us may take if we wish to correct our faults or make the best use of our inherited deficiencies, and in this context I view the teaching of the right side dominant individual as perhaps the most difficult task that any golf instructor can face. I say this because invariably, the instructor himself is a unidextran and it is almost impossible for him to understand fully the difficulties that most of us lesser mortals face. "Never teach a monkey to sing, it wastes your time and annoys the monkey" is a motto that I am sure many of the high reputation teachers subconsciously follow as they bypass the poorer players and confine their tuition to the better performers. Incidentally, these better performers (i.e. the unidextrans) are much better taught by simple skeletal or mechanical advice alone. To attempt muscular advice could be a great mistake and it is in this context that I believe a lot of tournament professionals and their advisors are presently going astray. A tournament professional who has been successful is unlikely to have a muscular component defect, and I am sure when they have a slump advice should be limited to simple set-up skeletal advice alone and mental support to rebuild confidence – not as seems to happen these days where swings are totally rebuilt. Sandy Lyle, Curtis Strange, Ian Woosnam, Seve Ballesteros and many, many lesser known names are surely living proof of the folly of attempting to tinker with muscular components that have already proved themselves in the field of battle. One hears that Colin Montgomerie is supposed to have a very amateurish swing technique. All I say is – good for the lad that he never changed it!

Very few of the really top class tournament golfers I have spoken to about my views have given me full backing for the ideas I have propounded in this book. Most say they hit strongly with their right hand at impact and feel this disproves all that I say. I think not! I would agree with them that they personally feel that they hit strongly with their right hand and right side, but I would claim that it is power that is in fact controlled by their left side and not overwhelmed, as is invariably the case in the right side dominant individual.

In concluding this chapter I would like to express my hope that much of what I have said will bear fruit and be instrumental in giving both pupils and their instructors added information that will help both in teaching and learning about the golf swing. I believe that different groups of golfers do exist that have different genetic capabilities, and these problems must be understood and must be identified and treated individually; each must be taught according to his or her particular need. I am convinced it is folly to treat everyone as if they were one homogenous group that could respond to one particular teaching method. I would like to see club professionals become much more knowledgeable about the frailties of the average golfer and be given (which I hope this book does) an added insight as to why we are such incompetent pupils and some idea of how to circumvent these inadequacies to the levels that the golfer may wish.

Chapter 9

Perfect But Imperfect

Once grasped, a theory can appear to be very simple – but as we all know, the execution can be a much more difficult problem. While I hope the reader has now reached the stage where he knows what the conventional golf swing is, and how he might move towards it, it must be realised that not all of us will reach the same levels of competence, however hard we try. The role that the mind plays is often of greater consequence than the actual swing itself.

Because we are human beings it means we are flesh and blood, and our ability to concentrate, co-ordinate, cope with stress or possess that mythical quality termed "feel", will vary from day to day. The mere possession of a competent swing technique is therefore insufficient in itself to play good golf; much more than that is needed if we are to compete with the best.

At the top professional levels how often do we read in the press that young "so and so" has top class potential but as time goes by we hear little or nothing of him again. How many "Rookies of the Year" have disappeared almost without trace? All maybe good swingers of the club, but living proof of the fact that much more than a competent swing is needed to make the grade at the top levels of the game.

Much the same applies to the club golfer and each of us at our own level of performance will fare rather better or worse than our swing warrants, depending on our mental approach to the task in hand.

At the upper echelons of the game the ability to have complete control of one's emotions must be the factor that, above all others, reigns supreme. I would single out this as the one factor that must separate the men from the boys or the good golfers from the really high earners. It has to be the icing on top of the cake.

Emotion can be defined as an agitation of the mind, or strong feeling, aroused by any internal or external factor which gives rise to some form of physical expression. In golfing terms this can be translated into anxiety about opponents, scores, putts, hazards, crowds, noise, or any of the other internal or external agencies that impinge upon us, and this anxiety will give rise to physical expression which will be revealed in the form of a reduction in the quality of muscular co-ordination.

Muscular tension is the great self destruct button of the golf swing. I have already stressed the need for muscular relaxation, particularly around the shoulder muscles, for without this there is little chance of the shoulder ring muscles working effectively and initiating the vital link between the two skeletal units. However well balanced a swing may be, if there is muscular tension present, then there is no chance of a powerful shot being hit. The individual muscles cannot relax fully and therefore they cannot contract fully when that time in the sequence comes about. Extra effort tends to be used as a compensation mechanism and a miss-hit invariably results.

Illustrations of this damaging effects of stress and tension in golf are legion and golf history is littered with examples. One has only to reflect on the last few holes of any Major Championship, or remember the palpitating play over the last few holes of the Ryder cup at Kiawah Island in 1991 to see the effects of stress on ability (I do not refer to Langer's putt – that was an error of judgement, not a failure due to stress). No person watching the putt of Doug Sanders at the 18th hole at St Andrews in 1971 in his attempt to win the British Open Championship will ever forget the smooth controlled-looking practice putt and then the rapid and hasty stroke with which he eventually hit the ball. Compare this with the putt of Jack Nicklaus at the 18th Green at Royal Birkdale in 1969 wherein the whole Ryder Cup match was at stake. If he sank it, the cup was retained, if he missed, it was lost. Both putts of extreme importance in their golfing lives. Nicklaus obviously coped with the stress that fraction of a degree better, or at least he did on the day, and at this level of competition that is what divides the Master golfer from the first class performer.

Confidence is the supreme controller of stress, and each and every successful golfer will have his own way of boosting his confidence. Arnold Palmer, for instance, was most confident when he was going for his shots while Billy Casper was apparently the opposite. Arnold Palmer's book "Go for Broke" explains much of the tensions within the game of golf, and throughout the book he gives examples of his super-optimism coming to his aid time and again, keeping tension at bay and allowing him to bring off the shots that were required. If Palmer attempted a conservative approach he found doubts crept in, putts were missed and shots strayed at the vital moments. The aggressive, optimistic approach suited his temperament and it allowed him to control his emotions. This was not so with Casper or Hogan; their emotional control was better the more conservative their approach. For them to have indulged in "going for broke" would have been disastrous and this was never shown more clearly than in the 1966 United States Open Championship when Casper caught up 7 strokes on Palmer on the back nine by playing conservative golf. Palmer, unfortunately for him that day, was also attempting conservative golf – for him it was the wrong approach and he dropped too many shots as the tension rose. Nick Faldo is another golfer who has learnt to control the stress he experiences, and throughout his career he has developed methods that help him to keep his confidence high. He has left very little to chance and he has done his utmost to ensure that his environment and indeed his whole routine of life are such that it enables him to keep control of his emotions and deal with the stresses as they arise.

There are also other ways of controlling stress. Familiarity with the experience is one, absolute belief in one's swing method is another. Of immense help to many are religious beliefs and strong support of family and friends. There is no doubt that success breeds success and with each success will come increasing confidence. A few golfers will unfortunately take the wrong path and resort to the refuge of drugs. Of these I suppose alcohol is the most common. In anything more than minimal amounts it will have adverse side effects and reduce co-ordination ability. This slight loss of co-ordination may at times be offset by its enhanced calming effect and the muscular relaxation it induces, and I suppose in moderation alcohol could be said to be the poor man's substitute for religion, philosophy of life, happy family, confidence in one's ability, have it what you will. I am certain there may be many golfers who do actually perform slightly better because of a moderate intake before a game.

I remember an example of this type of thing being played out before my own eyes. A few years ago two club members were preparing for the final of our club championship. One of them, a golfer who had represented his country at national level, was out on the practice ground swinging away. The other, a very able player, but strictly in the amateur mould, was in the bar preparing in his usual way. Confidence boosted, fear banished, stress controlled, he went out to win a handsome victory.

The point is that each was doing the norm for himself and each was pursuing the method he was familiar with for allaying tension. I am sure if the winner had gone to the practice ground instead of the club bar, he would have been thrashed out in the country.

The real hazard with drugs for the serious golfer is that they are not a long term solution, they can and invariably will be overdone and adverse side effects will appear. A rather extreme example of this once happened to a friend of mine playing in the final of the Far East Air Force Tennis Championships. It was the first time he had made it to the big occasion and his nerves were so shattered he felt it was unlikely he would do himself justice. It was at that point that he hit on the brilliant idea of taking an amphetamine tablet just before the final. He later told me it was the most fantastic experience he had ever known. He had never played better tennis in all his life, his co-ordination, power and control were supreme. He simply swept through the match, then leapt the net to shake hands with his astonished opponent.

The record book shows he lost 6-0, 6-0, 6-0 and barely won a point. Certainly he had banished the fear and anxiety he had dreaded so much, but the trouble was he had also banished awareness and co-ordination, although he himself was blissfully ignorant of the fact at the time.

Quite apart from the control of stress and its unsettling effect on co-ordination ability, it is an everyday experience for all of us to know and realise that our co-ordination ability varies at different times. It varies during the day and it differs from one day to the next. Any person whose job involves delicate co-ordinated movements knows that some days these movements may be precise and meticulous, yet on the next they are unable to achieve the same dexterity. There seems to be little rational explanation for this as fear, anxiety, tension and drugs are not involved and these are everyday tasks.

Research into body rhythms, biorhythms or circadian rhythms as they are called, has revealed that the body has a regular rhythm and indeed many individual parts of the body possess their own rhythmic cycles. For example, sleep is necessary once every twenty four hours, we know the female sexual cycle is twenty eight days, the heart beat, the respiratory rate, they all have their rhythmic cycle. It can be appreciated that there will be days when all these glandular functions and rhythms harmonise beneficially and these will be the days of peak performance and well being. It is on such days that the top golfer wins the Open Championship or the club golfer achieves his handicap cut.

An example of this type of thing was seen in Ian Woosnam's performance in the World Matchplay Championship at Wentworth in 1992. For two days Woosnam was invincible, he annihilated the opposition and was well under par each round. Come the third day it was not the same man, he lost out in the country. His explanation was that "he could not find the slot". I am sure this is just another way of saying that his muscular balance and co-ordination had not peaked that day and he found he could not perform at the supra-normal level that was required. This type of thing happens to all of us, but our off days are much more extreme – and much less important. The top golfers may have smaller variations but it is still sufficient to be reflected in an unsettled round and ensure a day when they have to put extra reliance on their short game.

A more recent example of this in action was seen in the play of Greg Norman on the last day at Augusta in 1996. I do not believe his loss of form was due to nervous tension, although it must have played some part as the round progressed. I believe that what we saw was the marginal loss of right/left side muscular balance. It is evident he had not been playing well the few weeks before the Masters and had missed at least one previous cut. My surmise is that during the subsequent practice sessions before the Masters he found the left side muscular control that brought his game back on track and the result was that during the first two rounds at Augusta he could hit the ball with supreme power, accuracy and control. To me, it seemed that his muscular balance was again beginning to slip to a marginal right side dominance during the third round. However, on this day his short game managed to hold things together. By the fourth day I suggest his right side musculature had taken dominant control and, in effect, he lost the exact bottom point of his swing arc. I believe his muscular balance had in fact moved a degree or two to the right and the release point of his arc correspondingly moved forward some one or two inches from the first two days. This minute muscular imbalance was all that was needed to induce the slight pull or push to his shots that made his round such a nightmare.

There is little any of us can do to achieve peak days of physical well-being when we most desire them, but there is certainly a lot that we may do to destroy them if we are not careful. The intake of drugs such as alcohol, sleeping tablets, and many other chemicals may alter rhythms. Alterations of time and sleep patterns upset the delicate balance and this is a hazard our top golfers experience more and more as they jet to all parts of the globe. But having said this, it never ceases to amaze me how well our top golfers perform just hours after they have flown the Atlantic or the Pacific.

Most successful golfers have long realised the benefits of not destroying their regular rhythms and it is no coincidence that the necessity of a settled and regular social and domestic life style has been stressed by the men who have made it to the top. The young tournament professional living it up – wine, women and song every night – may be having a ripping time but however talented he may be, he may as well give up any idea of being a world beater if that is his life style. The rhythmic disturbances will invariably catch up with him and the peaks that are so necessary for his continued success will be constantly eroded.

For any young professional, an over sized ego will give him an excellent start in his career because of its effect in boosting his confidence. However, if for any reason his ego becomes deflated he may well find he has little else to fall back on and his game will suffer accordingly. I believe this is one of the principal reasons why we see so many young stars rising rapidly from the amateur circles, producing the goods for a while, but once the bubble of confidence bursts they have not the depth of character, nor the life style, nor the deeper knowledge of their swing technique, nor the emotional stability to cope with the situations of crisis that inevitably must occur.

The inherent characteristics that we possess are the vital ingredients in determining the use we make of any God given talent that we possess. Our determination to succeed, our ability to sustain concentration and our inner emotions such as greed, stubbornness, pride, envy and ambition will all be crucial factors in determining how well we get on with the genetic muscular and skeletal material that we have been given.

Determination to succeed is something that every aspiring golfer must have in abundance. Crisis points will be reached in every round and it is at these points that inbred determination to succeed will become the vital driving force that will overcome these crises. Many players may be extremely skilled in swing technique, but if they lack the essential determination to see things through and they are of the character that gives up at the first sign of "Lady Luck" turning against them, I am afraid they will never make the most of their muscular potential.

Concentration is closely linked with determination, and high credits in this direction are required. I suppose Nick Faldo simply has to be the modern day supreme example of absolute unremitting concentration. In former days it was Ben Hogan who was given the accolade in this direction, but both men undoubtedly possess almost superhuman powers in this respect. Each of us at our own level will need to work on this aspect of our game.

Intelligence will, in some part, determine what use we make of the skills we possess. Some golfers are a bit short on I.Q., others are not. Average intelligence should be all that is required (though some might even dispute this). I am quite certain an I.Q. of 150 is entirely unnecessary and I believe it is more likely to act as a detrimental factor in attaining the top levels of golf. Despite what I have said in this book, remember that paralysis by analysis is a fact at any level of the game!

What use we make of our intellectual capacity is very much determined by our other characteristics such as greed, stubbornness, pride, envy, ambition and our personal interpretation of the game – all play their part. A great friend of mine, whose intellectual capacity is high, but is noted for his occasional flashes of stubbornness, came out with a perfect example of this one evening last summer. On this particular evening he had some private theory working for himself, but by the 14th hole it was painfully obvious to both of us that it was not the correct one as while he pointed his left shoulder towards a solitary cow in a field on the right hand side of the fairway the ball departed from his club in a perfect parabola and headed towards the bramble and gorse bushes on the left hand side of the hole.

I pointed out to him the need to relax his whole address position, to realign his framework and to desist in his five knuckle left hand grip.

He stood in silence, thinking deeply and taking all my advice in. After a lengthy pause he said in quietly measured tones, "good thinking, good thinking" and then to my utter astonishment he slowly proceeded to line up again with the cow in the field and as sure as night follows day, he proceeded to belt another ball deep into the whins on the left side of the fairway.

A more perfect example of stubbornness overcoming intellectual prowess you couldn't have wished for, and needless to say, with the fourth ball of his round he tried a more orthodox stance and achieved a measure of success.

I am sure most of us can think of numerous occasions when such emotions have affected our play. How often have we ruined our scores going for shots our intelligence tells us are just not on? Hundreds of time I am sure. The result matters little to us as amateurs (and it is exciting and necessary to do it on occasions), but if it is one's livelihood I am afraid such indiscretions, if indulged in too often, can see the end of a promising career.

In much the same context I have two close personal friends who have their own individual interpretation of the game of golf. Essentially, it consists of power off the tee - and only thereafter, is it a matter of getting on with the game as designed by the R&A. Now, when I say power off the tee, I really do mean power off the tee and anything approaching consistency and accuracy is eagerly sacrificed for the all-out maximum effort. It can be amusing to watch them playing a singles match, the meeting places are tees, greens and the 19th hole. Rarely do they have the opportunity for convivial conversation round the rest of the course (I hope they still remain close friends after reading this!).

An optimistic outlook on life is also an essential requirement and I would guess this has to be a common denominator of all successful golfers, be they professional or amateur. The most perfect example of this that I have come across was in the story they tell about Lloyd Mangrum who won the US Open in 1946. In his later years he suffered from heart problems and before he died at the young age of 59 he had endured 12 heart attacks. As he was recovering from his seventh he learnt that his golfing pal "Ike" Eisenhower had just had his second heart attack. Lloyd sent him a card wishing him well and a speedy recovery and reminding him he was five up on him. (Now there's a golfers optimism for you – the guy didn't even appreciate that he was actually five down – not five up!)

The conclusion to this chapter must therefore be that there are a multiplicity of factors that affect the control that we as golfers exert over our muscular motors and in the end it will be this multiplicity of factors that will separate each of us at our own level of competence. It is for these reasons that many excellent swingers of the golf club may never achieve the rewards they seemed destined to reach. It is also the reason why many golfers, who have apparently crippling swing defects, defy what would seem to be their limited ability and consistently perform well above what experts predict to be their capability.

Therefore everyone will have his or her problems. The reasonable swingers (i.e. the unidextrans) will have their problems of control of stress and emotions and intelligent guidance of their game. They will also have to cope with the minor left/right muscular variations that I believe change from day to day. However we, the club golfers, will have all this, but we will also have the extra and additional burden of finding a half reasonable swing before we even start to worry about the mental factors affecting our game. If we do eventually manage to find and achieve a reasonable swing, then we must hope that we have reasonably high credits in all the additional factors in order to keep control of our somewhat artificially acquired swing. It is as if we, the handicap golfers, have been given a standard saloon car to compete with, whereas the top performers have been given the Grand Prix version. Some of us will be able to upgrade our saloon a bit and find reasonable power and control, others amongst us will not, many will give up. But the point to remember is that quite a few Grand Prix drivers will find they are completely unable to control their high powered model and if the truth be known, their frustration will be just as intense as (or even more intense than) ours at the other end of the day.

On looking back on all I have said in this Chapter, it's maybe quite nice at times to be an incompetent club golfer whose livelihood does not depend on so many factors gelling together at the same time! When things do go wrong and we are having a bad day, it's perhaps always worth reminding ourselves that every golf shot makes someone happy!

Chapter 10

Personal Opinions

In this final chapter I indulge myself in some of my personal opinions about golf and at the same time try to answer the remaining questions I posed in the introduction.

The Perfect Swing

Throughout the book I have been careful to avoid using the word "perfect" to describe any golf swing. Instead, I have used the phrase *"Theoretically Ideal"* or the word "conventional". The avoidance of the adjective "perfect" is deliberate for the simple reason that I believe there is no such thing as "The Perfect Golf Swing". It is a concept more than a reality.

In the best of all worlds, "The Perfect Swing" should be capable of hitting the ball the maximum length possible, it should also be capable of total accuracy and absolute ball control; and in addition, it should be repetitive over and over again. The swing that should fit this description might be expected to be the swing that I have called the *Theoretically Ideal* swing, being as it is, a combination of the Y set-up with an absolutely centralised unidextrous muscular component. This "best of all worlds" combination ought to allow every muscle to be utilised to its maximum potential with an equal and opposite muscular action incorporated which would provide perfect balance, full power and reciprocal action. With everything maintained in the mid-line it ought to be a swing that would be readily reproducible and therefore capable of extremely consistent play.

In this context I regard Ian Woosnam as being the professional that is perhaps the nearest to this theoretically ideal concept. However, even he has problems at times with being repetitive. In fact, very few tournament professionals play with anything remotely near a Y set-up

134 *Personal Opinions*

and virtually all the players who have reached the top, and even those that have sought further improvement (such as Nick Faldo, Curtis Strange and Tom Watson) tend to adopt a Reverse K set-up position.

I remember once hearing of an amateur international player who played with the Y set-up swing. As part of the perks of international selection he was offered the best coaching that was available at the time. This is some years ago now, but the coach (with quite obviously misplaced enthusiasm) changed this player from his Y set-up to a Reverse K, and sad to say, he was never the same player again. A classic example of a mature golfer who was working at "his" perfect muscular and skeletal harmony level, but was damaged by a well-meaning but completely misguided attempt to inflict a preconceived idea of "Perfect" on something that was already near "Perfect" for that player.

My own personal view is therefore that "The Perfect Swing" is not an entity but is a range of swings, and each and every golfer will have his or her own "Perfect Swing" within this range. This will be the best combination of that person's muscular and skeletal component that will produce a functional and repetitive swing method.

With this definition Lee Trevino could be described as having "The Perfect Swing". I believe this to be true, and I also believe that if Lee Trevino were to move away from "His" version of "The Perfect Swing" and he were to attempt to conform to some idealistic concept, then it would require him to alter his muscular left/right side balance and technique to one that would be alien and false for him. I am certain that if he had been forced to go along this avenue in his younger days he would have been a good player, but he would never have achieved the degree of expertise he has done. I am sure the same is true of many other top golfers who possess slightly off-beat swings but yet are successful at the top levels. If these golfers were to give up what they already have achieved and stabilised, and start to search for "The" perfect swing, I think they would rarely achieve it. Most of them, by going down this path, would move away from what is – and I contend will always remain – "their" perfect swing. I am convinced this is the reason why so many good golfers deteriorate rather than get better when they initiate swing changes.

So we have the somewhat paradoxical situation that while there is an ideal concept, there is also ample practical proof that most of the swings that succeed at the top levels do not conform to this concept of perfection.

Tom Kite and Nick Faldo are two modern golfers who have been particularly successful in modifying their natural swings and moving towards what they regard as "the" perfect swing. I suggest they have been able to do this because their swing changes have in fact required very little in terms of alteration to the left/right side balance of their muscular components. In other words, they have undertaken alterations that are more in the nature of "within", rather than "away" from their basic muscular balance. The changes they have sought have been more ones of technique and emphasis but still remaining very much within their natural muscular balance. They are therefore not attempting a radical change of muscular emphasis such as Lee Trevino might have to do if he were to move towards a conventional swing. Despite this, I am sure it has not been easy for either of them and in order to bring about their swing changes both men have had to undertake a comprehensive and in-depth study of their golf swing, and indeed, of golf swings in general. I believe it is this deep analysis, plus an implicit belief that what they are doing is correct, that has sustained them and allowed them to perform even better than before. I suspect that in the process of achieving these technical improvements to their swings they have had to sacrifice a fraction of their natural instinct and flair, and this maybe accounts for the minor tussle that still seems to exist on odd occasions between their natural instinct and their new swing technique. I rather suspect that the desire to emphasise a particular joint movement is deeply ingrained and is never fully eliminated from the muscular memory, and maybe that is the reason why we see the odd wobbles from Faldo and Kite on occasions. Fortunately for Faldo his fellow competitors have not always been able to take advantage of these minor lapses and his detailed knowledge and the inner confidence that he has of his own swing technique, has proved capable of surmounting these crises when they arise.

Therefore while both Faldo and Kite have been able to rely on knowledge of technique and hours and hours of practice to achieve their goals, I still suspect that they have had to sacrifice a degree of instinctive flair to do this, and in situations of stress and crisis where Faldo and Kite rely on technique, an old style Ballesteros would have relied on instinct and flair, and technique would have been of a secondary consideration. As history tells us, this method either works magnificently, or it fails miserably. It is therefore an interesting test of methods in pursuing "The Perfect Swing". I personally feel few will succeed in the way Faldo and Kite have done as I believe their way is as much a mental exercise as it is a greatly improved swing technique. They must get tremendous satisfaction, fun and stimulation from the challenge they have set themselves and I believe it is more the challenge rather than the change itself that is the ultimate driving force for these two golfers.

While Faldo and Kite are two players who have successfully introduced swing changes, others have not succeeded. I understand the left handed Johnny Miller, at the peak of his career, was a player who went along the road of seeking "The Perfect Swing". Unfortunately for him he could never quite find the goal he sought. Tom Watson and Curtis Strange are others who have moved away from "Their" perfect swings in vain attempts to achieve "the" perfect swing and perform even better than before. I am sure they are examples of the difficulties in adjusting to a slightly altered muscular component and applying the "mental override" button as it were, all the time.

One may ask, why do players who have already scaled the heights and achieved success, continue in their search for the ultimate swing? Common sense must surely dictate that it must be easier to make more money with the same swing. The answer is obviously a complex one but I am sure it stems partly from the current belief that there is an anatomical or mechanical solution to "The Perfect Golf Swing", and partly from sheer boredom.

While I feel these top golfers are mistaken in their aim, I do understand the reason why they do it. Once you have scaled the heights and are self sufficient in material wealth I find it easy to accept that most intelligent people require and look for, and seek out, a further challenge. One can appreciate that for so specialised a career as a tournament professional the easiest thing must be to attempt to perform even better than before. Hence, we see the endless quest for "the" perfect swing. It is also interesting to note that very few of the really great players have gone down this avenue – Lee Trevino, Arnold Palmer and even the great Jack Nicklaus have all sought their challenge elsewhere and have had the courage to stay with their slightly "Imperfect" swings and have reaped the rewards for consistency. In my view they were correct, they kept faith with "their" perfect swings and were not tempted by dreams of absolute perfection. The other side of the rainbow is not always what it seems!

The corollary to my philosophy on perfect swings is that I disagree with excessive pressure being put on any young golfer to make him conform to a standard mould. Guided as to basic principles – yes, but not made to believe that there is one basic movement that is "The Perfect swing". An extension to this thinking makes me wonder whether the modern American school of thought is not guilty of some clone type thinking in this respect and they are in danger of producing too many golf look-a-likes, many of whom will be working at a slightly false muscular level and in so doing will be stifling a degree of natural flair. Could this be the reason why the Americans are not winning all the honours in world golf as they used to and why European and Australian golf has held its own at the top levels over the last decade? I have no proof to support my views except to cite the examples I see. I suspect that if natural talent were left to mature rather than being forced in slightly artificial directions, we may see less consistency, but we would see more flair, instinctive and exciting golf. Remorseless concentrated grind is undoubtedly one way to play golf, but is it the best way?

How does all this relate to the rest of us who are side dominant individuals? It is obvious we cannot think or work at the same elevated levels as the professionals. We have inbuilt into us a muscular component that is little short of a disaster for the purposes of playing scratch golf and we therefore have no option if we want to improve, we must go some way along the mental override path of attempting to harmonise our muscular and skeletal components and playing our golf at an artificial level, but somewhere in the functional zone (Fig 35). I would say that pupil and pro should maybe experiment with the Mindy Blake/Lee Trevino style as it may prove to be the most effective approach if we do not have the near perfect golf swing musculature built into us. Compromise will be the name of the game for us club golfers, but in my view there is no reason why it cannot be quite a reasonably effective compromise.

Pitching and Putting

Golf is a composite of two games and my dissertations so far have concentrated almost solely on the long game. It would therefore be an incomplete text if I did not afford some reference to the short game.

In this aspect of the game there are many amateurs who, with a little more practice, could more than hold their own with the average professional. However, put these same club golfers 150 yards or more from the green and they would not even be quoted in comparison to the professionals however hard they practised. The reason for this discrepancy in skills is that the club player is most likely a right side dominant individual but one with extremely good hand/eye co-ordination and he is playing all his short shots and putts entirely with his right hand in control, and little or no body action enters into the shot. These golfers are turning their short game into something akin to underhand bowling.

The problem facing such a golfer is – does he stick to what he feels is natural and works for him from 30 yards into the flag (even though he knows that a similar style of shot is not going to be effective for his long game), or does he attempt to master a new technique for the long game but retain his old technique for the short game? Professionals (except in rare circumstances) do not do this, they tend to use one method for all their play. This may vary from a shoulder controlled and stiff wristed putting method to that of a rather wristy putting stroke, but they do tend to show consistency throughout the whole range of their shots. Bob Charles is a good example of the first style with his smooth shoulder controlled swing with no accentuation to any part of the sequence; he carries this method forward throughout both his long and short game. Billy Casper, on the other hand, favours a wristy putting method and he also carried this over into his long and short game. This means that in both cases their putting stroke is a low power muscular test of their previous or next shot, be it a drive, an iron or a pitch. Bobby Locke was another golfer who demonstrated continuity of action throughout his game. He closed his stance and drew all his woods and irons, and he also adopted a similar technique for his putting.

So the problem is, does a club golfer adopt a right side dominant technique for the short game and a more conventional and left side controlled technique for the medium and long game? My view is that little harm is done with this division of labour provided it is a conscious decision. If the truth be known, this is precisely what the broom handle putters are already doing as they have their right hand in complete control of their putting movement. So we see, even professionals can on occasions use different muscular methods for their long and short game. Nevertheless, if a player is in mental override and is attempting to keep the left side in control throughout the long game, then I believe it is useful to carry this technique over into the short game.

Some club golfers, whatever method they use, remain extremely poor short game players. Is there any way they can be helped? The answer is – not very easily, but the following comments may help to put things in perspective. If we look at our body's short game mechanisms we find it is made up of three components. There is a sensory input side where information from the eyes is fed into the brain. Secondly, there is the brain with its conscious and subconscious assimilation of the information that has been gleaned and the formation of decisions regarding the movements to be carried out. Finally, there is the output side, which is made up of muscles and their nerve links from the brain. The efficiency of this system as a whole is very precisely measured by an individual's ability to putt, and poor putting performances may result from defects in any one of the three component parts.

On the input side good eyesight is essential to putt well. This is partly dependent on visual acuity but it mostly requires a combination of good eyesight and good binocular vision. It is extremely important that our eyes transmit to our brain an accurate judgement of length and borrow. This is mainly an instinctive gift rather than an intellectual process but there is no doubt that experience and practice does help. It would be rare for any person with defective vision in one eye to be a good judge of the length of a putt, and in this respect, it is surprising how many club golfers do actually have visual defects that may cause little inconvenience in their every day life but are too disabling for the skills required in the short game.

Concerning the conscious assessment of the short game, this is partly dependent on visual proficiency, but to a much greater extent on intellectual assessment. Factors such as the slope of the green, the grain of the grass, the lie of the ball, the best club to use, are all factors that must be thought about, considered, analysed and decisions taken before the shot is played. Once the decision is taken (part instinct and part conscious thought), the third pathway, the actual execution of the shot, will depend very much on inherited muscular co-ordination.

A defect in any one of these three component parts will reduce ability at the short game, and the sad truth is that as we age, the ability of our eyes to judge length, our visual acuity and our muscular co-ordination diminish. We can do little about these deteriorating factors, but can attempt to make up for them by a more determined conscious thought process and assessment of the situation.

This has to be the approach for the club golfer who is not blessed with perfect eyesight or high muscular co-ordination, and it does grieve me at times to see the lack of intellectual assessment that goes into the short game. Very few high handicap players really get down to study the line of a pitch or putt or consider the other factors involved. Most are perfectly happy to blame their technique when it is in fact their assessment of the situation that is the root cause of their inability to perform well. Their putting stroke may be reasonable but they are just not consciously assessing the correct line to the hole. For these golfers there is little point in blaming their putting in a vague and general way, if in fact it is their intellectual processes that are at fault. It is important to put the blame where it lies and seek the correction at this point.

Golf Course Design

The design of a golf course is a subject that tends to provoke fairly heated discussion amongst golfers and few features of any course will come in for universal praise from all club members. The reason is not that we are all obstinate, cantankerous individuals, but that we are looking at design features from differing points of view. Not only do we view them from different age profiles, we view them from different ability potentials, and the proffered challenge stimulates different people in different ways. For all these reasons it would be surprising indeed if the young and the old, the ladies and the men, and the scratch and the high handicappers, were able to agree about every design feature.

A discussion regarding design features is therefore not so much a discussion of who is right or who is wrong, but is one of whose point of view ought to prevail on any particular golf course.

We all know of club committees who take it upon themselves to design alterations to their own courses, and the most favoured method seems to be to make a new tee which will add some twenty or thirty yards to the length of a hole. Now this may well make a hole more difficult and satisfy a quest for additional yardage and no doubt be approved by the scratch golfer. However, it is often done at the expense of ruining an otherwise beautifully designed hole for the average golfer and turning it from what was a test of accuracy and ball control into a rather less interesting test of power.

At the present time the game of golf seems obsessed with increasing the length of holes and courses and I think it is time the merits of this obsession with length were questioned. In this respect I welcome the recent innovation to rate all holes and courses for difficulty, but what we really ought to be asking ourselves is, what are the underlying principles of golf course design? Is length and accuracy the best test for all golfers? What tests do we wish to set? Who are we catering for: is it the average club golfer, is it the scratch man, is it the tournament golfer or should it be a mixture of all three?

In the professional game length, accuracy and God-like putting are considered to be the supreme test of golf, and this mix of requirements has proved to be self selective of the unidextrous, well co-ordinated, reasonably intelligent golfer who has good emotional and stress control and possesses average or above muscular bulk or skeletal size. Golf has therefore selected these individuals to be its Master Race and it has done this by stretching courses so that the average championship par four is 400 yards plus and some par five's can reach 600 yards. Professionals freely state that if they cannot reach all par five's in two shots they really have little or no chance of top honours.

It does seem to me a little unfair that the smaller man should be put at such a disadvantage. He may well have equal skills and emotional and stress control as his more muscular and larger colleagues, but because of his smaller stature he is in danger of being denied the top honours in the game. It is almost a case of the smaller (and less muscular) man having to be even more skilful than his taller or more powerful colleagues in order to reach the top levels.

Have we got our priorities wrong? Is it right that we should make our golfing idols, and give our rewards, to this genetically and physically endowed group? Is it fair that the slightly built golfer, who may be just as genetically endowed with the skills of unidexterity and co-ordination, who has got emotional control, who is intelligent, who has worked hard at the game – is it fair that this golfer should be denied the top awards of the game merely because he is smaller of stature? Should we not be putting the emphasis of professional golf more on unidexterity, co-ordination, intelligence and emotional control and testing these skills, rather than these skills plus muscle mass or a large skeletal frame? My point in saying this is that all these skills you have to work very hard to develop, whereas the framework and muscle mass were God given and require no effort to develop.

If one were to change the emphasis and reward skills alone then it would mean shortening championship courses a fraction, it would mean planning fairways in more detail, it would mean encouraging the faded shot, the drawn shot, the high flighted shot and the low shot. It would mean putting less emphasis on the driver or long iron, it would mean steering away from sheer length and moving towards accuracy, ball control and intelligent planning of a round. One would aim to make the professional pay a penalty for sheer length with no brains and force them into varying their clubbing and shape of shot on every hole.

It would be relatively easy to design courses which would put the premium on intelligent planning and control of the ball. One would envisage the introduction of even more hazards, be they trees, dykes, ditches, ridges, semi-rough or bunkers that would force golfers to think more about their tee and approach shots. One could even envisage there being two fairways to some holes – one fairway perhaps tempting a long accurate power shot rewarded by a short shot to the green, the other a shorter shot, but one requiring a controlled draw or fade, but again, rewarded by easy access to the green if well played.

The idea would be to keep options open to players all the time; they would constantly have to plan their play. Tee placing would be varied day to day depending on the wind.

Most championship courses are already set up along these lines. However, I am sure they could, with good effect, be made even better. The 10th hole at the Belfry is a good example. Why give the class golfer the soft option of laying a ball up short of the water and then pitching over? Why not try to force him into a fade and an attempt to hit the green with his tee shot. If he does not wish to, then introduce bushes and leave him at least 100 yards short of the water. There is no need for the initial tee shot to be of some 270 yards: it could be dropped down to 230 yards and a shot that has to be faded.

I dare say my suggestions, if acted upon, would set up a howl of protest and be ridiculed as an attempt to make golf gimmicky. I would however, hazard a guess that the main chorus of protest would come from the power men, as they have a vested interest in keeping the emphasis of the game on power and length. A recent Senior Scottish Open was a perfect example of this type of thing when the favourite moaned about the short length of the course. What he really meant was that the course wasn't long enough to give him an (? unfair) advantage over the others in the field. The plain fact was that the skills he displayed on this occasion were insufficient to let him win. Maybe this is what the paying public want, maybe they want the golfing heavyweights to be the top men. My point is that it is quite possible for them to have both at once if our major courses were more skilfully designed. But it would mean blunting the asset of sheer power, discarding the length of a hole as the principal feature and instead putting the emphasis on skill and control of the ball. The professional who can only fade (or draw) a ball, or belt it miles on an open course, does not, to my mind, deserve to be at the top of the tree.

How would all this affect the club golfer and the design of his course? We have learnt that the club golfer is not a unidextrous, supremely well co-ordinated physically powerful individual, though certainly his intelligence and control of emotion and reaction to stress may be every bit as good as that of the average professional. The club golfer has a unidextrous range, but it will be well below that of the genetically endowed golfer. If a club golfer can learn to play his golf at a damped down muscular level or introduce some skeletal modifications, then a functional golf swing may be achieved. It may not be classic, but it should work quite well.

The important point is that if the club golfer is to enjoy the subtleties of the game then it is important that excessive length is not forced upon him, as he is genetically incapable of emulating his idols at the yardages they achieve. On the other hand, he is capable of getting similar satisfactions out of golf if courses are kept shorter and are better designed. Nothing can be more boring or tedious for any golfer than being forced to play rounds off tees that are too far back and being left banging endlessly away with two wooden clubs at greens 400 to 420 yards away. Play at this level degenerates into a meaningless series of maximum length shots combined with an iron to the green and then hopefully two putts. Little intelligence is tested, skills are not put to use and length is the one factor that is constantly being asked for.

This should not be the essence of golf. Golf should be for the fit young or middle aged individual who has practised and studied the game and should give him a test of expertise with all the clubs in the bag. It should force him to try to control the ball and make him think his way round a course.

A good amateur course need have very few par four holes more than 400 yards, and 330 to 380 yards should be long enough for most. Rarely should a par three need to be over 190 yards in length and there should be many more in the 70 to 140 yard range. No par five need ever be over 500 yards in length. Dog-leg and semi-dog-leg situations forcing intelligent tee shots should be used far more frequently. Judiciously placed trees, bunkers and contoured fairways and surrounds should be used to test skills in ball control. Much more imagination should be used in flag stick placement and green design. Forward tee placement should receive much more careful thought and not merely be stuck at a convenient spot in front of the medal tee

My suggestion is to let the average amateur play golf in much the same manner as the professional, but with each competing at their own level of course design. I am sure if this could be done, it would bring a lot more fun and pleasure into club golf. It seems so wrong to design courses that suit the most genetically endowed individuals but leave the rest of us to wallow in our handicaps. Skill and control should be the premium – plus length on occasions, but not to the extent that occurs at the moment.

I do not suggest that such holes or courses do not already exist – they do – but my point is that they are rarely considered to be the models we should be aiming for. Bigger and better seems to be the guiding light, and to me this is sad.

The width of fairways, the height of semi-rough and the degree of rough between tee and fairway are all sources of controversy in many clubs. Fairways tend to be equally wide stretches of turf from tee to green? Quite right say many club golfers, we should all be given the same width to land our drives on, place our seconds and so on.

But I would question this. Would it not be better if we all had the same degree of arc available to us off the tee on each hole. This could vary from hole to hole depending on the amount of land available, but it does seem odd to me that there are holes where the low handicap man may only have a fairway some 36 yards wide at 240 yards from the tee (i.e. a 9 degree arc to hit into), whereas the shorter player has extra handicap strokes available to him or her and a fairway of the same width at 160 yards gives him or her something in the order of a 13 degree arc to aim into. Most courses even go so far as to narrow the fairways the longer you drive off the tee.

I would suggest that a fairway design, where no other dominant features such as bunkers, trees or water hazards etc are used, should set similar problems to each competitor off the tee. Fairways on these holes should therefore be cone shaped off the tee with 230 to 240 yards being the set arc on a 380+ yard hole. The angle of the cone will obviously depend on the land available, the contours and the particular challenge of the hole. It may extend from a generous 20 degree arc down to a nail biting 10 or 12 degrees. Semi-rough should be long enough to penalise a half shot but short enough to ensure a ball is easily found. Figure 41 (Colour Insert) illustrates a conventional par 4 hole with, on the left illustration, generous fairway width for the shorter players but only a 10 degree arc for the longer hitter. The lady golfer has an even more generous 22 degree arc to aim into. The illustration on the right is the same hole with the fairway cut to give an equal challenge from the tee to all players, but again, slightly more generous to the ladies. I feel cone shaped fairways off the tee should be introduced on more of our par four and five holes so the higher handicap players can be set the same targets that the lower handicap players face almost every time.

[I wrote this chapter some years ago and have left it unchanged as it still contains most of my up-to-date thoughts on the subject. However, I am delighted that over the last few years golf course design has incorporated much of these thoughts and modern design does vary teeing areas and green shapes much more than it used to and tries to make the golfer plan his play of a hole by introducing two or more options off the tee. Sad to say, the rigidity of medal course yardage requirements does a lot to undo the skills of the designer].

Handicaps

I regard handicaps in golf as a necessary evil. There is no doubt that the most enjoyable games of all are the head to head contests with no handicaps involved. I personally think we have tried to become over precise about something that is not capable of precision.

The question is always asked of those who criticise. "Can you come up with a better system"? Well, here it is. I am not sure it is better, but it is different and it relates rather more closely to the way other sports are organised. For example, you don't have 3rd Team Soccer or Hockey players playing the 1st Team. So why all the time in golf? I suggest each player is allotted a handicap category rather than a precise handicap figure. He then competes in his medals within his own group or category against players of comparable skills (not necessarily as playing partners). Players would get promoted and demoted to higher or lower category ratings instead of having individual figure handicaps.

I have mentioned that golf is two games in one and it is therefore possible for us to have different skill levels in each department of the game. My suggestion is to use this as a basis for category grouping.

I suggest that every golfer must return a minimum of 6 completed medal cards per year in order to retain a category rating and compete in any competition the next year. The medal cards would have two extra columns on either side of the score for the hole. In one column would be marked the number of putts per hole (it would only count as a putt if the ball was actually on the putting surface – greenkeepers would have to define this properly). In the other column would be marked only the greens that were hit in regulation or better.

From these two figures, taken over 6 cards, a fairly accurate assessment of an individual's skills in both the long and short game could be measured. The category rating could be reassessed every 6 medal cards thereafter.

From the average of greens hit in regulation and the putts per round a golfer would be assigned a Category rating of between 1 and 6. The figure of 0.4 would round down and 0.5 would round up.

> Category 1 – 12 or better greens in regulation
> 33 putts per round
>
> Category 2 – 9 to 11 greens in regulation
> 34 putts per round
>
> Category 3 – 6 to 8 greens in regulation
> 35 putts per round

Category 4 – 4 or 5 greens in regulation
36 putts per round

Category 5 – 2 or 3 greens in regulation
37 putts per round

Category 6 – none or 1 green in regulation
38+ putts per round

There would be flexibility between the short game and the long game. The number of greens in regulation would be the principal category determinator but the number of putts could shift the category up or down. Every 2 putts less or more per round would count as one more or less green hit in regulation (as with greens in regulation, the number of putts would round up or down to the nearest whole number). These figures would relate to a S.S.S. course of 69 or 70 and a modification would have to be introduced for a higher or lower rated course.

Example. A player in Category 4 with an average of 4 greens in regulation but averaging 34 putts per round would move up to Category 3. An average of 37 putts would leave him in the same Category.

I would envisage only the Category 1 Group having actual handicaps and they would be much the same as at present and worked out to the decimal point and related to C.S.S. They would therefore determine their own C.S.S and not have higher handicap players, perhaps artificially adjusting it for them as happens at present.

No one apart from category 1 would have an actual figure handicap, only a Category. All stroke play competitions would be off scratch within your Category.

A cross category match play formula could easily be worked out – something in the order of 2 strokes for the first Category difference and 3.5 for each succeeding Category.

Such a system would change the emphasis of golf overnight from the current obsession with yardage and decimal points to one of the skills of the game hole by hole. No Returns would be a thing of the past as there would always be something to fight for. I would envisage there being more intra-Category competitions rather than inter-Category ones. I feel the present handicap knock-out competitions are exceedingly false as it is not really skills that win ... it is more the size of the handicap difference and victories at that level can be extremely hollow indeed.

I appreciate that the above is a bit of a "flight of fancy", but I do think the present match play handicap system whereby full difference is given is a complete nonsense and most single figure handicap players have lost a lot of interest in playing in such competitions. Because I think head to head matches without strokes is a far more sensible a match, I would make the suggestion that if we stuck with the present handicap system then at least we should experiment a little and where the handicap difference is within 3 strokes then the game should be played level. If the difference is within 4 to 6 strokes then again level, but with the lower handicap player playing off the back tees and the higher handicap having the advantage of playing a slightly shorter course off the front tees. If the difference is 7 strokes or more then both play off the back tees but three-quarters of the difference must apply.

Equipment

Club design and ball construction is constantly changing and the goalposts of improving technology are shifting all the time. This is as it should be, but it brings with it the fact that we, the ordinary club golfers, are continually being encouraged by the manufacturers and their marketing agents to buy each new gimmick as it comes along, with the hidden threat that we will be left behind in this technology revolution if we do not participate. Ironically, at the same time tournament professionals are arguing that the ball and club design has now outstripped the length of most courses to cope with the distances the ball is hit. I must admit that I think very few of us lesser mortals would agree with their observations and I am sure most of us would be delighted with a bit of extra length on top of what we already have.

Of the new advances, the peripherally weighted irons and woods have undoubtedly given us superior striking for shots that have not been hit in the dead centre of the club face. They would seem to be a must for the handicap golfer. The variety of shafts with their different flex is also a great boon to the ageing golfer. All this technology is much more scientifically presented to us than it ever was before. Ball design has improved dramatically over the last decade in respect of the dimple arrangements and the materials that have been used. They have given us a range of balls that vary from long distance lumps of concrete to almost rubber balls that we can manipulate around the greens. I have no doubt there will be many more improvements to come in the future, and each, no doubt, will be trumpeted across the pages of our golf magazines as the ultimate advance in golf technology and something we cannot afford to miss. The nature of things being as it is, we will be sorely tempted, and many of us will succumb. But be assured, each new, so called, improvement will cost a bundle more than the previous version! Oh that our handicaps would come down in the same ratio that our costs go up!

So be it, these are just the facts of life, we will have to accept them as money must be made in the market society we live in today, and new advances (whether they are real advances or not) will have to keep appearing. Nevertheless, with all these improvements, past and present, there is one further advance I would like to see introduced. I would like to see club selection put on a more objective basis rather than the slightly haphazard and subjective affair it is at the moment. I would like to see irons designated in degrees of loft, degrees of inset or offset and degrees of so called lie angle, rather than the simple 1-9 numbering we have at the moment. We already have degrees of loft for wedges and woods and I therefore see no particular reason why this should not be extended to cover the complete range of irons. If this were done it would then allow us to purchase the clubs we wished to make up our set and not have a predetermined ten irons thrust upon us. I see no reason at all why a range of a particular set of irons could not be manufactured in 4 degree loft intervals which would allow some 14 clubs per range to be available. This might even be reduced to 3 degree intervals from the 40 degree loft upwards for some of the more popular sets. Such a move would allow the golfer to make up his or her set much as they pleased and would stop the current habit of being sold a complete set of irons one may not really want (or require). There is little doubt that most of us would benefit from fewer clubs, but a better chosen range.

In addition to degrees of loft I think there is also a market for clubs to be clearly marked as being either exactly square set or a certain number of degrees either inset or offset. The inset or offset factor is something that is rarely talked or written about, but I personally think it is more important than we realise and is a crucial factor in club selection if all the range of side dominance in the golfing fraternity is to be satisfied. Clubs with different club lie angles are supposed to be available at the moment but little is done or discussed if you buy a new set. In summary, I would like to see far more trial clubs available for the club golfer from his professional, clubs that could be used for a round or on the practice ground. Buying a new set of irons is an extremely expensive exercise and if something like our clothes can be made to measure, so also I believe, should sets of clubs.

To some extent I have to agree that this is already done but in my opinion not nearly enough is made of it: the length of the shaft, the lie angle, the flex of the shaft, the degrees of loft and the inset or offset factors are all crucial as to how well an individual may hit the ball given his particular muscular/skeletal match. Once determined, these facts should be recorded and thereafter that golfer will be in a much better position to know the type of club and set of irons he or she might look for in the future. All quite simple to do but it requires time and effort from the club Pros, and the manufacturers. Are they prepared to do it at no extra cost? I sincerely doubt it!

Tuition

I hate to say it (but have done so a few times already in the book) that I believe tuition at club level has failed to keep pace with the times and has got itself into a bit of a rut. The standard pattern is for a club golfer to approach his professional and book a half hour lesson. They go to the practice ground and the pupil hits a few balls while the professional watches. Various positional changes will be introduced and the correct sequences of the swing will be stressed. The pupil will then be encouraged to go away and practise and book another appointment for review.

Any marked improvement in a golfer who has played the game for some time is, as we all know, very unlikely to materialise.

I suggest this approach now needs an update; it is too limited and old fashioned and really must be looked at anew. I would like to see Club Professionals, encouraged by their members and committees, being far more active in their teaching and instruction roles. I feel they must be allowed to sell themselves and their skills to better advantage and be encouraged to do this by their clubs, they must not wait for things to happen. I see no reason why Club Professionals should not (for a nominal charge) present one or two club evenings each Winter or

Spring where they discuss the golf swing, discuss the full range of equipment, talk about swing weights, shaft flexibility, golf rules and decisions, and all the multiplicity of things that fascinate the club golfer. Video analysis of certain members' swings would be a guaranteed success (provided the members are willing)! Interesting film or video material could be shown by courtesy the PGA, giving insights into the previous year's tournaments or material that would otherwise never see the light of day. All this I am sure would be fascinating to the club golfer and I am certain there is a wealth of material available that ought to be available to the Club Professional that is not on general circulation.

I feel the interest in such evenings would be tremendous and the club professionals could not fail to reap a harvest in lessons and equipment if they were well run events and the professional knew his subject in depth. I appreciate many club professionals may not have the expertise to hold an audience by themselves for an evening, but colleagues could help out and the home Club Professional could add items of club interest and gradually build up his skills at presentation. There is no doubt that if this were to come about professionals would need to be backed up much more by the PGA than they seem to be at present.

The question of tuition of the golf swing, as I stated earlier in the book, is for professionals and not for me. However, I have tried to outline the reasons why, as club golfers, I believe we are such poor performers. I personally do not believe real improvement for most of us will come about until our teachers understand and appreciate the workings of our muscular component and how it links with the mechanical movements, and the vitally important part it plays in determining the swing technique we end up with. Improvement, or even alteration for the better, does requires that the muscular component be matched to the swing technique or, on occasions, the swing technique be matched to the muscular component.

Until we get away from the belief that there is only one correct golf swing and that anatomical or positional teaching is the only way to teach or reach that golf swing, then I fear we will not move forward very much.

I appreciate that professionals do modify swings rather than rebuild them as they often consider it to be too difficult (or not in the pupil's interest) to attempt to radically alter something that has been established for many years. However, the pupil may actually want a more classic swing, but the dilemma for the Pro is – how can this be done in a few lessons? I personally feel the way forward is by the pupil intellectually understanding the roles of the muscular and skeletal components. Once this is understood, then the pupil and the tutor can intelligently discuss every aspect of the lesson and both will know precisely the path down which they wish to go. In other words, read and digest this book and then – what the pro tells you – will make a lot more sense as there will be understanding with it.

The teaching of youngsters I regard as a special category and outwith the above comments. I feel they should all be taught the conventional swing and the Reverse K set-up initially. I personally would stress relaxed muscular balance and a full shoulder turn as the most important aspect of any swing. A percentage of youngsters will respond and show promise, a larger percentage will not. If they do not, yet remain keen, then is the time to analyse the reasons why they are not improving and maybe assist them towards a modified set-up and swing technique that will be more suitable to their individual muscular component.

Epilogue

It is my hope that both the amateur and professional golfer has found something new and interesting in my book. I hope it has filled a gap that has existed for too long between tuition and results. If I stimulate a new approach to the game I am satisfied. If I improve the reader's play, I am even more satisfied. If I have assisted the Professionals in their difficult task, I am exhilarated. On the other hand, if I have given either group frustration and anguish, then I have failed in my purpose. But remember, at the end of the day, it's only a game. Or is it?

ILLUSTRATIONS.

CHAPTER 5

CHAPTER 5A

Figure 27 A,B,C.   *A. Unfolded swing set-up.*
B. Shoulder ring turning – spiral twist of body muscles from the top and start of two rod flail angle developing.
C. Body power muscles poised and balanced – shoulder ring turned and two rod flail angle developed.

CHAPTER 6

Figure 28 A,B, C.D.   *A. Hip movement as swing initiator.*
B. Shoulder turn as swing initiator.
C. Wrist cocking as swing initiator.
D. All capable of the same top of the swing position.

Figure 29.   *Right side dominant swing – the breaking of the three constants.*
Right side dominant action in the muscular ring breaks the base of the flail 1st rod (coat-hanger) and with it the integrity of the triangular form and the grip. The reduced power is then right side orientated and delivered at the wrong site.

Figure 30 A,B.   *A. Too much weight on the right – will be forced to "hit from the top" and end up falling back at impact as 30B – bent left elbow.*
B. Falling back at impact due to right side dominant musculature in control. Flail point in front of the left foot where right arm and club are in alignment.

Figure 31.   *Flail point in a right side dominant swing – either Y or Reverse K set-up.*

Figure 32.   *Effect of left side muscular bias on flail unit.*
The three constants of the 1st rod are maintained with left side muscular bias in the Reverse K set-up.

Figure 33.   *Flail point in a left side dominant swing if Y set-up initially.*

Figure 34 A,B.   *A. Trevino style set-up – Reverse K and slightly open stance.*
B. Trevino style impact position – left side of flail in firm control.

Figure 35.   *The range of muscular and skeletal components that combine to produce "A Perfect Swing".*
Range of skeletal set-up's from Y to Reverse K (plus Trevino like adaptations) that will produce a functional swing. However, both muscular and skeletal components must be in harmony.
Range of muscular component that best fits with the Y to Reverse K set-up is from perfect unidextrous to all the left side of the unidextrous range, i.e. the four left-hand side columns of Figure 3A-P29.

156

GOLF
– THE PRO'S DON'T
KNOW IT ALL

BY NEILL WATSON KERR

This publication is available from bookshops, newsagents and sports outlets or can be ordered from the following address:

Bieldside Publishing
Hallam Grange
2 Golf Road
Bieldside
Aberdeen
AB15 9DD

UK customers please send a cheque or postal order *(No Cash)* for £8.99 plus £1.01p postage and packing (allow additional £8.00 for each copy. Post and packing included).

Overseas customers please allow £2.50 postage and packing for the first book and £9.00 for each additional copy: post and packing included.

Please supply .... copy/copies of "Golf – The Pro's Don't Know It All"

Name (Block Letters) ....

Address ....

....

Total Value of Order Enclosed